Long Days
Late Nights

Frank Keating

Illustrated by John Jensen

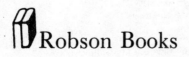Robson Books

The author would like to thank the proprietors of *Punch* magazine for their permission to reproduce the illustrations in this book.

FIRST PUBLISHED IN GREAT BRITAIN IN 1984 BY ROBSON BOOKS LTD., BOLSOVER HOUSE, 5–6 CLIPSTONE STREET, LONDON W1P 7EB. TEXT COPYRIGHT © 1984 FRANK KEATING. ILLUS-TRATIONS COPYRIGHT © PUNCH PUBLICATIONS 1984.

British Library Cataloguing in Publication Data
Keating, Frank, *1937–*
   Long days, late nights.
   1. Sports – Anecdotes – Facetiae – Satire – etc.
   I. Title
   796'.0207   GV707

ISBN 0-86051-293-2

Typeset by Preface Ltd., Salisbury, Wilts and printed in Great Britain by Biddles Ltd., Guildford.

Contents

Foreword

Punch had not, until Frank Keating, engaged a regular sportswriter. There were established Fleet Street prejudices in support of that attitude. Sport has long been relegated (good sporting word) to the back pages, where literate readers need not necessarily be affronted by the writing of men who, all too often, treat both the performers who are their subjects, and the readers who are their customers, with a contempt which verges on – or transcends – bullying.

Not to deal with him in negatives, Frank Keating has retained into his adult writing years an almost boyish enthusiasm for sporting performance, and a completely non-envious admiration for its performers; and he enjoys sharing his pleasure with his readers. His is the blend of romanticism, relish and sheer delight, which is the sporting enthusiast's reaction to the close – or vicarious – watching of the playing of games.

It is significant that Frank Keating's earlier book, *Another Bloody Day in Paradise*, an account of the 1980–81 MCC tour to the West Indies, is, beyond doubt, the cricket tour story closest to the players and, for that reason, unlike all others, most readable, and one they most admired.

Of course, because he is Frank Keating, he is not embarrassed – but proud – that, when he was young – and not so young – he collected the autographs of great players; and we may bet that he still has them safely stored away among the vast, motley shelves of sports books he has not the heart to throw away.

It is clear that sports-writing is not – or should not be – important in the pattern of literary life: just as sport is not – or should not be – important in the shape of world history. The fact remains that many unimportant – and important – people retain a deeply romantic and nostalgic feeling for the sports, and the great sportsmen, of their childhood, and abiding interests and loyalties in the sporting events of today.

Frank Keating caters for them. *Long Days, Late Nights* provides memories and relish within games; a simple pleasure in the unimportant – or are they? – sporting activities of the human race.

Let us not be over-grave about him. He enjoys, almost extravagantly, shares, and communicates his simple – but deep – pleasure in sport and its performances. It has been said that despite his position in the 'quality' press, Frank Keating handles sport with the common touch: it should be added that he brings to it warmth, humour and distinction. Good health, much laughter and enough seriousness, in your delights, Frank.

J.A. 1984

Introduction

I once sat awestruck in the England cricket team's dressing-room in Barbados when Sir Geoffrey Boycott was taking off his armour after being shatteringly bowled by Michael Holding for a duck. I once sat on Muhammad Ali's massage table immediately after a fight as the *nonpareil* explained to me – his fist almost brushing my jaw – how to left-hook a southpaw. I once spent a convivial, sherbert-sucking half-night on a barstool in India with Ian Botham before he went out in the morning and scored one of his power-crazed centuries – in forty-four minutes. I once discussed the art of Pele with Bobby Charlton as we helped saddle-up his daughters' gymkhana horses. I was once leaning on a golf bag marked 'NICKLAUS' as the blond bear himself was wagglingly squaring up to a golf ball on the 18th tee at St Andrews in the last round of the Open. . . .

Honest.

That is the traditional McEnroe-confided-in-me-yesterday manner in which to introduce a collection of sporting reminiscences such as this.

But this is not that kind of book.

John Macadam, great and good and generous pioneer sportswit and columnist, once advised that the only way any hick of a hack could get away with the totally undeserved grandeur of an anthology like this was to insist that, with half a dozen strokes of the typewriter, you forced the alteration of the offside rule in soccer, got *Wisden* burned in the public square of Melbourne, and instigated the de-sanctification of the Lawn Tennis Association.

Nor is this that kind of book.

It is, if you like, an overgrown schoolboy's adventure book, by – and for – an enthusiast who has been incurably hooked for life on reading newspapers from back to front. There are a lot of us about.

The random hotchpotch of pieces are reprinted here exactly as they were written for *Punch* – dashed off to dead-heat the deadline, ripped out of the 'writer, and just pipping the day's last postman to the red letter-box. Phew! That's that for another week! Apart from dotting a couple of i's, the plan has been to help the essays retain whatever spur-of-the-moment freshness they had. That also means, therefore, that they retain their slapdashed inaccuracies. So don't all write in at once. I have never been too hot on finicky, frindling, facts and figures. I hope, simply, that the book might qualify as a good in-dipper, a bedside friend that might first keep you up late and then send you smiling to sleep.

I started these weekly columns for *Punch* a couple of years ago, with allowance to take a day off from my beloved *Guardian*. I have had overgenerous encouragement from two enthusiasts and sports lovers, those journalistic actor-managers, Alan Coren, editor of *Punch*, and John Samuel, sports editor of the *Guardian*, for whom it has been a pleasure to write – and to drink, gossip, and laugh with. Sincere thanks, as well, to that kindly genius, John Arlott, for his Foreword, and to Angela Oram for shuffling the higgledy-piggledy cuttings into such attractive order.

Every week, as the magazine has plopped onto my doormat, the drawings of John Jensen have been a delight and glossed up my pieces far beyond their deserts. Gratitude, too, to every sportsman involved as I've loitered on the fringes of their big times; also to all provincial and Fleet Street colleagues for their quips and quotes, their company, kindness and, not least, for their cribs.

F. K. 1984

PLACES

Monsignors and Mounties

As kids we were taken once or twice in the old Ford Prefect to the Cheltenham races in the early springtime: over the top from Stroud past Painswick and Prinknash. It all seemed perfectly innocent adult fun: it must have been, for it was well supported by the clergy and my father kept doffing his cap to dog-collars. The horses had nice comfy gymkhana names like Prince Regent and Sheila's Cottage. In the paddock they would look like a Munnings picture, cool and smooth and colourfully silky. At the end they would be heroic and knackered and steaming, and their toothless jockeys would be clapped into the enclosure and would tug their forelocks to the grateful gentrified locals before scurrying off with their mud-spattered tack. And we'd get home in time for high tea and Uncle Mac on 'Children's Hour'.

Little did I know.

A couple of years ago, in this famous third week of March, I was sent to interview two leading Irish steeplechase jockeys on the eve of the festival. We arranged to meet over a drink at the George on top of Birdlip Hill. A drink! We started at seven. TWO jockeys! The whole of the weighing room seemed to have turned up for the ride. Each had his confessor, his personal padre, by his side.

Well past midnight, with a notebook crammed with gloriously unusable quotes from both the broth and the cloth, either a monsignor or a mountie – by then there was no telling which was which – suggested a wee putting competition on the carpet of the hotel lounge. A putter and golf ball materialized and an empty beer mug was laid on the floor some thirty yards off. Right, lads, what's the stake per putt? I fingered a forlorn back-pocket fiver. They agreed on fifty quid per putt – first one in takes the lot. I made an excuse and collapsed. Next afternoon my two jockeys won a race apiece.

Steeplechase jockeys may be in the same sort of game but actually they are as different from the sallow, tight-cheeked, waxwork midgets of the Flat as, well as the buccaneering, bucolic Botham is from Tavare – that worried Jeremy Irons of cricket who seems in a permanent inner torment about whether to play forward or back, to revisit Brideshead, or to look up that bint some Frog lieutenant left behind in Lyme.

To the nation, from David Coleman in his Aintree titfer to Granny Giles with her hat-pin and fifty pence each way, the Grand National might seem to be the whooping end-of-term beano for National Hunt racing. And it sure is one helluva pagan festival: yet to the real fancy the National represents just a cheery enough lucky-dip sideshow; to those in the know the Cheltenham festival is pontifical sung mass on the high altar.

In 1977, a boyo came over from County Meath and inside three weeks won the Cheltenham Gold Cup *and* the Grand National. Says John Burke: 'Coming into the winners' enclosure at Cheltenham on Royal Frolic was the greatest moment of my life. It beat winning the National. The Gold Cup is the Blue Riband, the one every jockey wants . . . but then, to win any race at Cheltenham gives you an incredible feeling. Mind, you need a heck of a horse to win, so many run out of petrol as they come round that final bend and up the hill. But for those who make it, the roar of that crowd is a fantastic experience.'

What with rugby union championship, Cheltenham races, and St Patrick's Day, March is the month for brogues. In the Irish Catholic Church, Lent relents. Over come the clergy by plane and train, their breviary in one pocket, *Timeform* in the other. They could print the racecard in Latin at Cheltenham. *Jonjolius O'Neilliensis.*.

Mark you, Cheltenham races and the Catholic Church have been saddled up a long time now. A lively settlement of Irish

Romanies found refuge and work in the new spa town when they were thrown out of Paris after the French Revolution. And when sporty Captain Berkley founded the horse-race meeting below blissful Cleeve Hill in the early part of last century, the Irish became the grooms and ostlers, and then started bringing over their relatives, who in turn took to bringing over their own nags to join in the fun. And most of them stayed. Indeed, a hundred years ago Cheltenham parish church had to build itself a new cemetery for, as the old refrain had it:

The churchyard's so small and the Irish so many.
They ought to be pickled, sent back to Kilkenny.

Other churchmen, high and low, would still say aye to that. They always have. Cheltenham's mighty bible-thumper, Dean Close, loathed the town's horsey Irish more even than drink. 'Papists, gambling and profligacy,' he raged in 1835, 'are essential concomitants of horseracing.' No joy either from the scribbling jockey, Cobbett: 'Cheltenham on race day is the resort of the lame and lazy, the gourmandizing and the guzzling, the bilious and the nervous . . .' Actually, seeing he mentions it, he'd find things hadn't changed much. But no! Hey ho, for three days in March what a darling jig the Irish bring to the prim place that calls itself the Queen of the Cotswolds. Not that the residents stir much once they've locked up their dogs and their daughters. But shopkeepers wear greedy, greasy grins, and hoteliers in a fifty-mile radius are, as they tell you smugly over the telephone, 'in a No Vacancies situation, I'm afraid'.

Doubtless, some without a bed will look to seek sanctuary in the local Catholic churches – and play at a little putting up the aisle till dawn, and occasionally light a candle for guidance from the Sacred Heart. Oh, dear Lord Jasus, should it be Bregawn or Silver Buck for the Gold Cup? And what about Dickinson's other two, Captain John and Wayward Lad? Should I have each way for the lot, 1–2–3–4, what d'you think, Lord? An' what d'you fancy yourself, sor, for the Champion Hurdle? Can we take it as a sacred sign that Jonjo's decided to get aboard Ekbalco, though I must be

13

honest with you, Lord, I've always been rather inclined to Royal Vulcan meself: did y'see the grand sight of him finishing at Leopardstown the other week; oh yes, sor, of course, y'would have . . .

It is, in the end, simply the Innocent God-fearing versus the Flaming Bookie. Like Jeffrey Bernard's gloriously true tale of the time he saw an old Irish farmer put one hundred pounds on a horse at 7–1. The bookmaker's sign on his stand proclaimed him to be a Mr Finnegan. When the horse obliged and your farmer had his 700-odd counted into his gnarled palm he kept saying, 'Yes, you've heard of *Finnegans Wake*, well this is your fockin' wake, Finnegan.'

Wind Assisted

You read it here first, preen, preen . . . I quote this column's brazen introduction on the eve of the opening matches of the Five Nations' rugby union championship: *'I must report my irresistible hunch that Scotland are going to win the thing outright for the first time since shorts crept above the knee.'* They had not won the Triple Crown for forty-six years, nor achieved the Grand Slam for fifty-nine. But so it came to pass.

Another triumph for the simple back-pager's rule – 'In a two-horse race always tip the outsider.' No-one remembers when you forecast the favourite. As that kind, good, and pioneering pop sportscribe, John Macadam, demanded just before his death: 'On my tombstone I want just the sentence "Here Lies the Only Man who tipped Farr to beat Louis," and the lower down, below the cross and among the lilies, I want it carved "And on my card Farr Did Beat Louis".'

It's only when, from the top of your head, you rattle off the McLitany of names, that it seems astonishing that Scotland have not trumped the table in almost sixty years. MacEwan, McHarg and McLeod; Robson, Rollo and Rae; Dick, Deans and Dorward; Stagg, Steele, Smith, Stevenson; the Laidlaws; Irvine, Waddell, Broon o' Troon, the 'Mighty Mouse', and the 'Epony-Mous' himself, the flaxen wraith, Ken Scotland.

The mythical trophy is won for beating, in the same season, the three other British sides (if France are included in the full hand it is the Grand Slam). Scotland's tawdry record throughout my lifetime is the more surprising when you know

15

England and Ireland to have been extremely easy meat just about every other year, with Wales not much tougher, except for that dynamic decade when Gareth delved and Gerald ran, and Barry was the gentleman.

Certainly on the mid-Saturday of March the only place to be was Murrayfield. The hooley that night was something terrible and glorious. Whole new meanings were given to the phrase. 'A pint of Tartan, please.'

And the traditionally staid, pinch-lipped elders of the Scottish Rugby Union opened their first bottle of champagne since 1925. They also allowed their players, as soon as the final match was over, to come out of the showers and be presented with a hideously garish necktie, badge bristling with thistles amid the braided legend *Scotland's Grand Slam.*

This had obviously been ordered well before the game. There's confidence for you. Also generosity, a commodity often given short shrift by the Scottish RU. For instance, before the Grand Slam 'final', I spent a day with Dan Drysdale, one of the five octogenarians surviving from the legendary Scottish side of 1925. Recalled Dan: 'The night before the deciding match it was bitter cold in the North British Hotel in Edinburgh. I was sharing with Herbert (Waddell). We asked a chambermaid to make up a fire. Inside a week we both had a bill from the Scottish RU for ninepence!'

That has been the Scots' trouble over the century of international rugby football. Too gentlemanly. Too amateur. May the best man win. It may be something to do with the ferocious nationalism stirred up by the Hampden soccer Jocks, but the old school tie has only just been loosened up at Murrayfield. Indeed, it comes as an awful surprise to see the new, swish and sponsored grandstand ringed with advertisement hoardings. This would have been unheard of at the Scottish RFU only a few years ago. Though, when I examined them, seven were for whiskies and two for porridge oats, so I suppose the committee co-opted some sort of advertising standards officer from their own ranks.

Throughout the century, the dour conservatism of Scottish public school ethos has dominated the game up there. When manual workers from the Border mills took up the game in the late 1800s, the gentlemen from Edinburgh were banned from playing them. Once, one do-gooding gent did travel down to referee a workers' game, but returned, all shook up, to report, 'It's not an umpire those people need, but a missionary!'

Not till after the First War did the Scots allow a new ball to be used in their internationals. Too expensive. For years they held out against printing match programmes. For a long time the Scottish RU refused to allow players to have numbers on their backs, the easier for any spectators to identify the participants. 'My office requires me to deal with a rugby match, not a cattle market!' exploded the legendary SRU autocrat, J. Aikman Smith, when Twickenham hesitantly suggested it.

When some long-ago, pioneering sponsor from the City of London offered to put up a tangible trophy to represent the Triple Crown, an aghast Scottish committee minuted that 'Such a suggestion even sullies the welfare, reputation and purity of our game.' They didn't mind the Calcutta Cup, contested annually by England, for that was melted down Indian silver, commissioned by Scottish officers and gentlemen serving in Calcutta. No profit involved.

And when they went on the warpath, the SRU was uncompromising. In 1912, a small ad appeared in *The Scotsman*, 'S. W. France: Bordeaux club require capable stand-off half-back. Good position assured in local wine business . . .' With such vigour did the Scottish rugby establishment pursue the issue that they had the President and Secretary of the Bordeaux RFC officially banned from even watching rugby for life! Though I don't suppose the French took much notice.

A few years earlier, Scotland refused to let any of their players tour New Zealand with the 1908 British Lions – for they had heard that the All Blacks' touring team to Britain in 1905 had been given an expenses allowance, to buy their food, of three shillings a day. Sixteen years later, still shocked, Scotland refused point-blank to play the mighty All Black 'Invincibles' of 1924.

The legendary Jock Wemyss played for Scotland both before and after the First War. For the first match of 1919 the newly demobbed soldier arrived at Inverleith. All the other players were being issued in the locker-room with their new

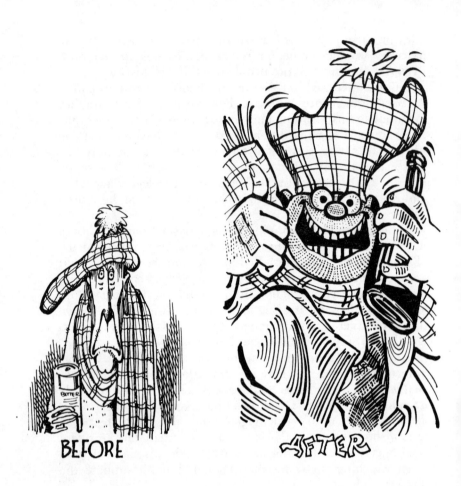

BEFORE

AFTER

blue shirts. There were only fourteen. 'What about me?' asked
Jock. 'You were issued with yours in 1914,' came the reply,
'don't say you've gone and lost it.' He had to make do with a
pale blue, working man's job.

It was only fifteen years ago that the beanpole lineout
merchant, Peter Stagg, was seen with a tin of black boot
polish, moments before running out at Murrayfield. He was
'inking-in' two gaping holes in his stockings. The SRU only
issue one pair of stockings per season. Otherwise you buy your
own.

18

In more ways than one, this historic season has seen dear old Scottish rugby carried, kicking, into the second half of the twentieth century. And yet in some ways, nothing's changed. Edinburgh's first international was played at Raeburn Square 'in front of eight thousand people who braved a wind of many gusts', according to the contemporary report in 1878. Sure as eggs, those winds are there still. It was good to be walking to Murrayfield again. After the traditional warming snorters at the match-morning mingle with the mob in the foyer of the North British Hotel, the streets of the grey, gaunt city were full of men and boys aiming in only one direction. Nobody else seemed to be about as, already, a misty midday was turning fast to a muffled teatime gloaming.

There are more mustering, clustering schoolboys at Murrayfield's rugger, often hand-in-hand with solemn-walking men down from the hills, with china-white Scandinavian complexions and pale and knobbled knees below thick plaid, travelling-rug skirts. These locals stand upright to the gales. Sassenachs walk as though the mufflers round their necks are weighted with lead: bent almost double, like a crouching hooker in the scrum, into the teeth of the winds. (Bernard Levin, an old hand at the Edinburgh Festival – and that's a summer celebration – once complimented the ancient founding father and City architect on inventing hang-gliding long before the sport was given its name!)

And those zephyrs were *really* zapping at last in favour of Scotland's international rugby side.

Tide and Time

So the Cambridge Boat race crew were water-logged even before the start of the race. There is nothing new under this watery, late winter–early springtime Saturday, Surrey sun . . .

Very first kerfuffles had been about professional coxes. These languid, pre-Victorian athletes could heave-ho in jolly boating weather, but expected gnarled little paid watermen to steer 'em, to read the tides, dodge the ducks and miss the moorhens. Some didn't like mixing with such skiff-raff. Like C. J. Selwyn, of Leander, who ranted in his Boat Race dinner speech of 1839: 'The true way to make my office unnecessary is to allow no waterman to have anything to do with our matches, but to leave it to gentlemen. I do not wish to say a word against watermen, but watermen's ways are not our ways, nor watermen's notions our notions.'

The old pros chewed their gums and hung on. A dozen years later there was a more public blast for caste. Tom Egan, a former Cambridge blue and coach, had by then become editor of *Bell's Life in London*. In 1852 he wrote: 'Our favourite science, rowing, ought to be the first object of our love. . . . the chief end of these great contests of ours is to exhibit to the world rowing in perfection; whatever tended to lower style or to diminish aught of the beauty and polish of the perfect eight-oar is to be resisted and condemned . . . and the Universities do neither wisely nor well in allowing watermen to touch the yolk-lines of their match-boats.'

The gumbooted, knowing boatmen had slurped off, cursing the gentrified slobs, long before 1868, when a crew seriously threatened to pull out of the race. Just before the day, on February 17, one of the Cambridge crew, the Hon. J. H. Gordon, died after shooting himself. Cambridge, in mourning, at once asked to withdraw the challenge. Oxford refused. Get this: the reason Gordon was such a hero in Cambridge was not because he was a stout oarsman, but because he had trained for the race by *canoeing* solo from Dover to Rotterdam via Cap Gris-Nez, the Saône, the Rhône, and the Mediterranean to Genoa, thence to Switzerland and on to the Reuss, the Dar and the Rhine.

I do not, I admit, hoard such heroics in my head to rattle off over leisurely towpath strolls. That one is cribbed from a truly spiffing history, *The Oxford and Cambridge Boat Race*, published by Stanley Paul and written by Christopher Dodd, that rare bird who can go about painstaking research with always a smile a'twitch on his lips. Dodd's new work is a relished and relishable labour of accuracy and love; he is a man with a beady eye for both the correct and the quirky, an ear for odd bods, and always an affectionate leer towards the loony. Like the aforesaid, the Hon. J. H. Gordon.

Not that Dodd actually encourages me or you to turn up to the Towpath on the day. Like the Blackpool illuminations, a century by Tavare or a 1–1 draw by Arsenal, the Boat Race might be worth seeing if you happen to be there, but not worth actually *going* to see. I have been twice – no, no, that's an exaggeration for you cannot really count a ten-second blink from the back of a very tall crowd in front of that pub near Hammersmith Bridge. Even then it gives the lie to that long doodle of cartoonists who have had us believe that Cockney urchins bedecked in blue scuffle around the towpath scragging each other and shouting 'Cymbreedge!' or 'Horx-ferd!' No, the live Boat Race crowd, such as it is these days, wear denim twills, smoke Whiffs by Wills, sup real ale in halves, and squire gels called Daffers or Poops.

On the other hand . . . When he proposed the traditional toast 'The PM' – not to the Premier, but 'Putney to Mortlake' – at the post race banquet at the Savoy in 1979, Harold Macmillan talked of 'the happy world' of his youth 'when one could go into some sports without having first to go into a long test to see if you were a man or a woman'. On Boat Race day, he said, everyone cared – 'everyone, the whole of London, the costermongers, the drivers of four-wheelers, those delicious Hansom cabs, everyone cared. All wore the colours, light blue or dark blue. In the household, great divisions, the housemaid, the butler . . . as a child I was Cambridge. Nanny was violently for Oxford. . . .'

Ah, the blissful days of youth! And as child Harold slept and Nanny kept vigil, wondering on Cambridge for the morrow, how were the Boat Race crews preparing? On the eve of the race a century ago, as the old blue, Guts Woodgate, recalled, the two crews entered into partnership for a cat hunt. 'Oxford were to find the cat; the dog was my terrier, Jenny. Cambridge was to supply the room for the sport. The tortoise-shell cost one shilling. She was given sanctuary in a big zinc bucket, and placed in the Cantab sitting-room in the old Star & Garter. The cat was as big as Jenny, but in due time, with a badly clawed nose, Jenny got her fangs into puss's windpipe, and hung on. Oxford had 6–4 the best of the partnership, for the Cantab room was so odoriferous next morning that they had to seek another apartment for breakfast! . . . I'm afraid one and all had no qualms of conscience; the cat was under sentence of drowning when we bought her, so she was *mutatis mutandis* only out of the frying pan into the fire when we gave her a run for life.'

Puss had a watery tomb that night. 'As a fact, she actually came back on the morning flood to reproach our cruelty just as we were launching. We could identify her without a doubt as she floated by . . .' Woodgate then stroked Oxford to a half-minute win in unjolly boating weather that wasn't fit for cats.

Grand Masters

I have never dared ask him to his face, but I am assured in the locker room that this is a true story: some years ago an acquaintance of mine in the west of England was due to get married: he was nutty about golf, a short but straight enough hitter off the tee and only inclined to panic, even club-throwing, when anywhere near sand or scrub. But he stuck at his game. His hero was Jack Nicklaus.

A few days before his Saturday wedding he happened to win first prize in the clubhouse raffle. An air ticket for one to attend the Masters tournament in Augusta, Georgia. The flight was to leave the morning after the ceremony. He said it was too good an opportunity to miss. His bride presumed he was joking – but, sure enough, after a splendid family reception and one night of the cosy connubials he was up early and away for his solo flight. When he returned a week later his wife had flown. He has never set eyes on her since.

Sometimes, when he's putting at the last and into a serene, shepherd's-red sunset over the Bristol Channel, he will pull from his bag a peaked cap bearing the flamboyant badge 'Masters 1972' . . . and every time he arranges it on his head with reverence he offers himself a tiny sigh and gives a momentary rueful shrug before settling over his shoes for the stroke . . . Trouble is, you don't know whether it's his wife, or Georgia, on his mind.

The Masters gets them like that. Though it is a comparative baby – in 1984 it celebrated its half century – the tournament

23

has long been an indisputable biggie in the fixture list of legendary sporting challenges. It has an inner calm, a sumptuous, stylish cool. The TV and radio commentators who deliver the goods by satellite each year all have to submit to a stern lecture forbidding mention of any other golf tournament ever played except the American and British Opens and their respective amateur championships.

Nor is money to be mentioned while the play continues – though a very handsome, gift-wrapped bundle of boodle will find itself in the winner's locker. No hint of advertising either inside or outside the grounds: one year a supporter of Arnold Palmer assailed the scene by hiring an aeroplane to fly noisily over the course all day trailing the banner GO ARNIE GO! The organizers wanted to shoot it down.

The Masters was founded by Bobby Jones who, legend demands, will remain probably the finest player the game has known. He retired at twenty-eight in 1930 after playing in only twenty-seven major professional tournaments – as an amateur. He won thirteen of them, and at the same time he gained university degrees in law, engineering and English Lit. He looked like Douglas Fairbanks, had the most chivalrous of gentle manners, and for the remainder of his life he fought with valour and from a wheelchair a crippling neural disease.

In 1930 a high-powered New York financier, Clifford Roberts, took the shining, young, renaissance, man-child champion to Georgia to see some real estate, an old indigo plantation which had been cultivated for a century – and with gloriously wild abandon – by a Belgian emigré family of horticulturalists called Berckmans. Roberts and a syndicate bought the property for Jones, and with a Scottish landscape artist, Dr Alistair Mackenzie, he built his 'perfect' golf course. Not that there was much work for the bulldozers. As Jones was to write before his death in 1971:

'I shall never forget my first visit to the property . . . the long lane of magnolias through which we approached was beautiful. The rare trees and shrubs were enchanting. When I walked out on the grass terrace under the big trees behind the house and looked down, the experience was unforgettable . . . indeed, it even looked as though it were already a golf course. . . .'

24

He and the Scottish doctor agreed on the two crucial
precepts: fit the golf to the land, not shape the land for the
golf; and make it a memorable round for both hero and hacker
alike. As Jones put it: 'Two things were essential. First, there
must be a way around for those unwilling to attempt the
carry; and, second, there must be a definite reward awaiting
the man who makes it. Without the alternative route the

situation is unfair. Without the reward it is meaningless.'

Putting it another way, he said when the course was opened in 1932: 'I hope it is perfect, for it is both easy and tough; there isn't a hole out there that can't be birdied if you just think; there isn't one that can't be double-bogeyed if you stop thinking.'

Jones and Roberts presented their masterpiece to the United States Professional Golf Association and asked if they would put the course on the rota for the US Open. They were refused with various fob-offs: they preferred 'ocean' courses, Augusta was at its best, 'azalea-wise', in April and the Open was always a high summer fixture etc., etc. It was probably jealousy as well as a niggle at Roberts buying himself in.

So they started a tournament of their own. The first Augusta Annual Invitational was held on March 22, 1934. Roberts' immediate idea had been to call it 'The Masters', but Jones vetoed it, feeling it would be presumptuous so to call a tournament of their own creation. Jones' modesty was always to curb Roberts' megalomania. Nevertheless, the Press got a sniff of the discussion and by 1938 Jones agreed to the official name. Later he was to worry, and admit, 'yes, the name was born of a touch of immodesty'.

The winner each year is made an honorary Augusta club member and awarded the right to wear the club's pale green blazer. He could – and still can – wear it off the club's premises only during his year as champion and only at social golfing functions. Thereafter it is kept for him permanently in a cedar-lined closet in the champions' locker room, where every champion has permanent privileges till death.

It's all good corny stuff from this distance. But the Masters at Augusta, fifty years on, has won itself such a hold in the legend of an ancient game that you scoff at your peril.

Golf – indeed all sport – retains an eye-lowered reverence, a religious solemnity, when hushed talk gets round to Augusta's green jacket. My friend from the west of England is just one of millions. He will stay up late each year to watch the finale on television. He will be alone at his hearth. I am as certain as I can be that he will contentedly sprawl his feet across his coffee table, sup a beer – and be wearing a battered, highly prized, peaked cap bought at Augusta in the week that he was married.

Derby Daze

Last May, in New Zealand, I went to the races. A trim little oval of whitewashed rails encased the paddocky scrubland on the plains below the long range of humpbacked Tararua Hills near Palmerston North. It was a day out for farmers and their families, shepherds and their dogs. Like a friendly point-to-point in the English shires, but with no trace of haughty accents or Harrods' hacking jackets.

A weatherbeaten, leathery-jowled old cove in a lumpen, friendly, overlarge, unpressed, green-grey suit twirled a huge arm around my shoulder. I had never set eyes on him before, 'What,' he asked, whispering in side-of-the-mouth conspiracy, 'd'y reckon for June One?' I looked as dazed as I felt 'Y'know,' he insisted, 'so tell me; will Sangster run Lomond or one of his others? Is Dunbeath what it's cracked up to be, and what about this thing called Gorytous?' I am terribly sorry, I said, I do not speak Maori and know not what you say, ''Course y'do,' he said, 'but I respect y' f' not tellin'.' And he winked.

Beg pardon, I said, but I have no remote or imaginable clue as to your drift. 'Gerraway!' he said – and in crescendo, 'June One. Epsom Dahns. *The Derby!*'

Ahh! the Derby. *The* Derby. No, I said, I only know the winners *after* the race. I'm not a betting man, though, yes, on June One I expect I'll have my usual quid on Lester. The old boy ambled off, disgusted, and into my brain galloped famous names in a higgledy-piggledy, coconut clatter . . . Sea Bird and Shergar, Henbit and Pinza and Morston, Never Say Die and Sir Ivor, Nijinsky, Roberto and The Minstrel . . . and on and on. Those last five, rattled off the top of my head, were, I realize, all ridden by Lester Piggott. He has won the thing nine times, a record that won't be surpassed. His ambition is to win ten Derbies.

The first Derby winner to canter into my consciousness was when I was eight. In 1946 a mottled grey rank outsider called Airborne was entered at 100–1. A flurry of bets by anyone who'd had anything to do with the wartime RAF Parachute Divisions brought the price down to 66–1 on the eve of the race.

The legendary old war correspondent, René Cutforth, once told a tale of that day. Apparently, René himself was one of a number of returning heroes who suffered a delayed shellshock immediately after their demob back to civvy street. He was sent, with others, to a nursing home to recover. No-one was exactly certifiable. Well, not till one poor chap in a cherry-red beret announced that he was determined to plonk his newly issued cheque for his Prisoner of War's back-pay – some £4,000 or so – on a mottled-grey, 66–1 outsider in the next day's Derby. Nurses panicked for him. Whitehall was telephoned. If only somebody could be found with enough stripes to certify him and so revoke the cheque, the 'madman' and his gratuity would be saved. Nobody was bold enough to make the decision without a memo in triplicate. It was too late. They were off! Airborne won, of course – and by teatime the 'nutter' had been discharged as totally sane. And also exceedingly rich.

The Derby! All of 'uman life . . . There's the posh part, plebby and debby an' toppered an' tailed. You must raise your hat to the Queen – but never cheer – and, in the paddock, mutter things like 'sound hind' or 'intelligent head at least', and all the while closely examining the meaningless numbers on your racecard. Then there's the sloping natural grandstand where they park the wizard-prang account executives in their open-topped Brighton buses. There you get totally plastered, and you still don't know who's won even after the 'News at Ten' that night.

The fairground side is pretty abysmal actually. But there's nothing tatty about Tattenham Corner. I love it there. Hog your place on the rails all morning, and commune with sun and wind and grass and olde Englande content and get generally cheesed off and bored – but then, around half-past three, witness the very nub of the race, note what is fifth round the turn, and unstraining, and there's your likely winner, see the frothing pant of the front runners who have already missed the boat, and be at one with that jockey who, narrow-eyed, high-bottomed and urgent, twigs the fractional gap the very moment they pass you . . . it takes about six seconds and then they're gone in a kaleidoscope of coloured caps and curses and an enthralling roll of thunder that shakes the earth. That's it. And it's ages till the name of the winner filters back down the Downs. It usually turns out to be the one that was fifth as they passed you. . . .

For the jockeys themselves, you fancy, the Derby at Epsom has never changed in over 200 races. More than half a century ago the famous old jockey-journalist, Jack Leach, wrote:

'I never rode a Derby that wasn't a bit like a polo match – only with more horses. By the six furlong gate, things have generally sorted themselves out a bit. The short sprinters have already gone, and the milers won't last much longer although they are already getting in the way on the descent to Tattenham Corner, which incidentally is a perfect turn for a horse and horseman. It's extraordinary how many die out just after they turn for home. I know the feeling so well, and in a way it's a kind of relief. You know you've had it and can do nothing about it. The thing then is to relax, stand up in your stirrups and watch the finish – if you've got good enough eyesight.'

Then the winning jockey might allow himself a smile as he dismounts into the barrage of camera lenses. Except Lester. It's just another day's work for that genius. He'll touch the peak of his cap with his whip to the owner's wife and that will be it as he hurries away to change into his silks for the next race. And, as he enters the sanctum of the weighing room, he will only hear a dull muffle of cheers. For Lester Piggott's deafness allows him to be distant and detached. Or so he likes us to believe.

One time, after one of his Derby wins, Lester was walking to his car at the end of the day. An old, bedraggled punter, down on his luck, approached the champion for a touch. 'You haven't got a couple of quid to help out one of your biggest fans, have you, Lester?' asked the old boy. Lester cupped his hand to his ear and said he couldn't hear him, it was too windy. The fellow dragged Piggott down to the shelter of a car and repeated the question – 'You couldn't spare a fiver to help out one of your biggest fans?'

Said Lester: ''Ere, you only asked for two quid the first time!'

Hooray Henley

The only good thing to relish about the last week of the Wimbledon tennis championships is that there is at least one day's escape – at Henley. Wimbledon these days is gruesome. The charms of Henley remind you what Wimbledon might have been a quarter of a century ago. Of all the world's supposedly unmissable sporting events, Wimbledon is far and away the most missable. It is not the same on television, I agree. You don't get the genuine flavour. Thank heavens for that.

Wimbledon is an unbearable scrum. It's either too hot or too cold. Never just right. As well as a collective pout of puerile players (and that's another story!) Wimbledon is the stench of sandals when it's wet, and of armpit when it isn't. It must be greed – as well as the grudging need to line players' pockets with prize money – that has the All-England club charging twice as many to get into their grounds as can possibly see a match in anything resembling comfort. Ten thousand have guaranteed seats for the afternoon: twenty thousand have to mill and queue about the concourse, pretending like mad they are enjoying themselves. Simply, I fancy, the smug fact of their presence keeps them in the esteem of the Joneses for the next 363 days. For sure, most Wimbledon watchers see nothing over the mass of milling millinery in front of them, nothing but the occasional overarm swish of racket by a very tall server.

All the while they are dodging the most surly, growling, band of uniformed hired hands from the military that can have been assembled this side of Moscow. And, as in Russia, they queue for everything at Wimbledon: they queue to get in and they queue to get out; they queue for the main courts, and for the ludicrously expensive, rip-off, strawberry tea. Policemen grin as they watch mugs queue to bargain with ticket sharks. Taxi drivers switch off their meters and charge what they like on the way from the station: there's a queue for that privilege, too. Certainly, at Wimbledon, everyone queues for the loos.

Gentle, blissful, happy, haughty Henley is one day's parole. No smelly, sardined District Line to the taxi queue at Southfields. Henley is the breakfast-stopper train from Paddington, a leisurely change at Twyford for that rattlety-tat, rattlety-tat, little swaying job that chuffs cheerily through the woods and water meadows of Wargrave and Shiplake. Sixpence for who sees the River first! There it is! Hooray! Hamper's full of champers! What fun we'll have today. What *leisurely*, lying-on-the-grass fun. The sort of fun Wimbledon provided in days of old when Billy Knights were bold and Robinson's Barley Water was actually served by Old Heathers and not by crisp, clipped, cocky coves from the Special Events Public Relations Department – and who are only there really to make sure the bottle labels under the umpire's chair face the TV cameras.

Henley remains unchanged; almost unchangeable. The *Punch* office invariably had its summer outing there. It should still. One hundred years ago to the week, Mr Punch, in the guise of Jingle Jnr., described the jaunt:

'Red Lion crammed from cellar to garret – not a bed to be had in the town – comfortable trees all booked for a fortnight in advance – Lion gardens crammed with gay toilettes – flags flying everywhere – music – singers – niggers – conjurors – fortune tellers! Brilliant liveries of rowing clubs – red – blue – yellow – green – black – white all jumbled together – rainbow gone mad – kaleidoscope with delirium tremens. Henley hospitality proverbial – invitation to 16 luncheons – accept 'em all – gone to none! Find myself at luncheon where I have not been asked – good plan – others in reserve! Houseboat like Ark – Joan of Ark in corner with Darby – who is she? Don't No-ah – pun effect of cup. . . .'

Such flavours will still be there as the Pimms and the Plymouth Pinks are ordered to a tinkle of glass (at Wimbledon everything's plastic) which matches the contented rustle of the larches and chestnuts which soar steep from the blissful river banks. Mind you, parts of Henley try to be frightfully posh. There are notices which mean 'No radios', but which actually say 'No Portable Wireless Receivers'.

There is also an order at the Stewards' Gate – 'No Perambulators'. This only means the kiddies' variety, for inside there are any amount of senile gents, all dolled up in tiny prep-school caps and shrunken striped blazers, being wheeled around in wheelchairs. Wheelchairs at Henley are not perambulators. By mid-morning, once the booze has started to whooze, all is serene, and the chinless, slack-lipped, tight-blazered, old buffers lose the fierce glint in their eye. They could all be auditioning for the part of Robert Morley's understudy.

Meanwhile, on the water, the clubs and the colleges stream and strain with symmetrical, rhythmic grace. The odd undergraduate on the towpath gets worked up. 'C'mon Jesus, for God's sake!' or 'C'mon Clare, pull your finger out!' But the rowing is just a backdrop to, a diversion from, the picnics.

It was always so. On May 20, 1839, the Cambridge crew and its supporters held a meeting at the Sun at which they tossed a gauntlet to Oxford to race them for Henley's Challenge Cup. The CUBC minutes record the consumption through the evening: '70 bottles of champagne, 38 of Moselle, 12 of claret, 17 of sherry, 57 quarts of ale, and £6. 7s. 6d worth of punch'.

That was Olde Englande content in midsummer. Before Mammon invented Wimbledon.

Links Men

I am a comparative newcomer to big-time golf watching. Over the years I have ruined many a good walk by enjoying a swipe or two, but I suppose it was being riveted by Tony Jacklin's exploits on television in the early Seventies that inspired me to pick up my brolly and watch. Since 1976 I have missed only one British Open.

I can remember vividly my conversion to the game on that third Saturday of July, 1969. (Everything finishes on a Sunday now, to accommodate American television scheduling). The crew-cut Jacklin wore purple trousers which were much too short for him. He had fallen asleep in a chair the night before and his US golfing buddy, Bert Yancey, had carried him to bed. As he walked up the final fairway on short little legs inside shorter little slacks, he was mobbed by the crowd and he lost a shoe. Calmly, he re-laced it, and sank the winning putt.

Next year I was in front of the set with my sandwiches. Doug Sanders also wore purple and had a tap-in for the title on the final green at St Andrew's. He addressed the ball, then neurotically bent down to brush away some imagined wormcast without changing the stance of his feet. I knew he would miss it then. He did – and then went for a long, lonely walk up into the hills. His wife found him talking through his gaffe with a herd of cows. Said Doug: 'I guess nobody wins the Open; the Open wins you.'

In 1972 at Muirfield, Jacklin wore a white shirt and now very expensive, tailored, lovaty-check slacks. He was skating home and Trevino did for him with a final bluster of unbelievable chip shots which he kept potting from the fringes of the greens. As they walked up the final fairway, Trevino turned and offered the young Englishman a gigantic, friendly wink. Jacklin grinned back. He knew he was only at the beginning of his prime and would be passing this way again and again. But he never did. Those crazy chips of Trevino's dispatched Tony back to the pack of also-rans.

Next year at Troon there was old Gene Sarazen's hole-in-one at the Postage Stamp. What television that made! And another little man, too, bowed into our sitting-rooms. Remember Mr Lu doffing his hat to all and sundry? Whatever happened to him? Perhaps his lack of English finally got him down. Once he tried to explain: 'I only speak Hongkong golf English. When I go professional I take teacher. Every day it is A-B-C-D, A-B-C-D. I say him, in golf no A-B-C-D, only 1-2-3-4, maybe 5. Perhaps I take new teacher, eh?'

The first time I was at the Open in person, Johnny Miller won at Birkdale. He wore yellow, and had a matching corn-stoop, blow-dried head of hair. He looked like a young Jack Nicklaus. He was a devout Mormon ('Praise the Lord and pass the No. 1 iron'), and said after his victory that he would actually rather have spent the week back home with his children. Perhaps for that reason, Miller never became the consistent champion that he had threatened to be during that blistering week near Southport.

At Turnberry in 1977 was played the most stirring challenge in history. It was not an Open Championship, it was a two-man, head-to-head contest between the monarch, Nicklaus, and the heir apparent, Tom Watson. After two rounds they were level. In the third they both shot sixty-five. There was no way they could keep it up for the final eighteen. They did. Me and a multitude followed them round. At the Ninth, still dead level, they both sat down at the tee and said they wouldn't continue unless we calmed ourselves. At the Fifteenth, as Jack seemed to be composing himself for the knockout, young Tom holed a long, long, chip from way off the green. Jack visibly reeled. He knew then the Gods had decreed it – 'the Open wins you'. At the end, Nicklaus' embrace of the new young champion was as genuine and generous and touching a thing as I can remember in all of sport. In the pandemonium, Tom whispered, 'So this is what it's all about?' Jack just grinned back; and nodded.

The following year Nicklaus won at St Andrew's. I appropriated a Press armband and, honestly, followed the great man, at a distance, up over the Swilken Burn's dotty little willow-pattern bridge and on up the Eighteenth to poor old Doug Sanders' hole. The big fellow walked in solo state up the fairway towards the world's most famous clubhouse, garlanded with affection like an emperor home from a ten-year crusade. I was twenty yards away, matching him stride for stride. You can see me on television whenever it's repeated. 'Hello Mum! Me and Jack, see! Up the Eighteenth at the Open!'

The cheers rose so thick as to make an almost tangible proscenium over the vast open-air amphitheatre. Nicklaus was wearing a sweater with an Oxford-and-Cambridge blue diamond pattern back and front. He waved twice to the crowd as he walked over the 'Valley of Sin' to putt. He said: 'I understand the Scottish people's feelings for me. And they know my feelings for them. They know my feelings for golf, for British golf, for Scottish golf and the very history of the game.'

The late, great, Pat Ward-Thomas wrote next day: 'When he walked up the Eighteenth, the warmth of acclaim that greeted him was as much, I believe, for the man himself as for the supreme champion of our age.' I can never tire of quoting a piece Alistair Cooke wrote many years ago about another acknowledged and heroic champion golfer, Bobby Jones. It surely applies to Nicklaus too: 'What we talk about here is not the hero as golfer, but that something Americans hungered for and found; the best performer in the world who was also the hero as human being, the gentle, wholly self-sufficient male. Jefferson's lost paragon: the wise innocent.'

Since that delirious day at St Andrew's we've had the young Spaniard, Ballesteros, and his glorious, uninhibited zig-zag in and out of the car parks at Lytham, and we've had Watson again (and again), and nice Bill Rogers carrying the ancient old vase back to Texas. But I'm afraid I can't help myself, and I'll be rooting for the big fellow, Jack, once more this year.

Unless, of course, Jacklin starts hitting those greens. Perhaps Tony should get himself another crew-cut. And look out those half-mast purple trousers.

FACES

Baron of Beefy

Sometimes in Press boxes I have been flabbergasted as one or two English journalists have seemed to be *willing* Ian Botham to be dismissed early. It's a good story, see. *Botham Fails Again! Botham Unfit! Botham Too Fat! Botham Won't Practice! BOTHAM MUST GO!* is far better stuff for their splash subs just back from the Fleet Street pubs than *Botham Saves England Again!* That's old hat. That's been done before. Give us something new, kid.

It is, as the actress said, difficult to know what piece to do next, dear. My friend Derek Hodgson of the *Daily Star*, a soft, erudite, gentle fellow till deadlines loomed, had the right approach. I sat next to him in Press boxes all through Botham's touching but haphazard stewardship in the West Indies a couple of winters ago. Plink-plonk in the sun, went leather on willow . . . all was tranquil in the shade as we dozed the day in deckchair's curve, or picked our nails, or played snap, or yawned and scratched ourselves, or pinpricked at pomegranates, or browsed through the obits in *Wisden*, or occasionally made a lazy note of the score to assist with our close-of-play drivel. . . . Then, of a sudden, Botham would, say, drop a catch no other man would have even sniffed, or someone would snick his bowling for four 'cos he didn't have a third slip, or he would be caught in the distant deep when a magnificent soaring steepler didn't quite carry . . . and Derek would extravagantly pick up the phone back to his office in England: 'Hold the first edition! New lead coming! – and snappily, urgently, he would wind in a new piece of white paper, poise twitching fingers like Rubinstein waiting for his cue from the podium, and then the Olivetti would woodpecker out the legend: BANANA BOAT FOR BOTHAM stop BRING BACK BREARLEY exclamation.

Memory diffuses reality. It never rained in childhood summers, did it? The heroes of our youth never had a bad patch, did they? Just to take three at random – look up Wally Hammond's tour of Australia in 1946–47, or Denis Compton's in 1950–51, or Peter May's in 1956–57. They could hardly lay bat on ball at times. All Botham's tours have been triumphant by comparison.

Botham has had to play much, much more Test cricket than that legendary trio. Every summer he can count on one hand the opportunities he has had to go out and build a County Championship innings for Somerset; and sharpen, and work on his technique. I'm not saying he would, mind you – just that he has had very few opportunities to do so, should it ever dawn on him to try. He remains gloriously instinctive, and should be treasured as such.

Drudge and custom have staled his bowling, they say. Nonsense! For his infinite varieties and bold con-tricks have all the best batsmen still cursing his extravagant guile as they

traipse from the wicket cuffing their pad with the bat. And which fieldsman in the world has a safer pair of hands?

He has had only one Christmas at home in the last eight years. He deserves one, to wind down, to recharge; to do a bit of rough shooting or coarse fishing; to play some Saturday soccer for his beloved Scunthorpe; to have more than a few Sunday noontime pints with his mates; then crash out in front of the television set or his 'classical' pops, before taking his pet boxer, Tigger, for a gallop across the moors in the teatime dusk. The solitary Christmas he did have at home is actually recalled with a sheepish laugh: 'It was a disaster; not only did I catch pneumonia but the police decided to choose Christmas Eve to serve me with a summons.'

The two sections of the nation who hold him in most esteem are his fellow players for England and Somerset, and every serving British schoolboy.

For he bats the way that small boys dream of. And schoolboys are very good judges: they think straight, they are bold, they are simple, they understand that heroics are sponsored by daring, they are unapprenticed to prejudice. Schoolboys also like men who hit the ball clean over the grandstand at Lord's just to get their eye in.

England's dressing-room name for him is 'Beefy', instead of 'Guy', as in gorilla, or 'Both', as in Scotch-*broth*, not *oath*. The Somerset opening bat, Peter Roebuck, says of his friend: 'Whether hunting, shooting, fishing, kicking, bowling or drinking, Ian resembles a baron of the wild, medieval days. He drives his car, as they rode their horses, with panache. His instincts are not tamed, his zest for life has not mellowed. His whole-heartedness leads to triumphs and troubles, to success and scrapes, for it is not balanced by a shrewd appreciation of public relations nor by a tolerance of rudeness or criticism.'

Peter recalls Ian's first ever game for Somerset: 'He announced himself by cracking three fierce boundaries before tamely offering a catch to short extra-cover. He returned to the pavilion in a cloud of dust, storming into the dressing-room to utter the oft-repeated words, "I should have belted the ruddy thing harder!" Most of us, upon being caught, regret having hit the ball in the air at all. Already Botham's only sorrow lay in not having hit it *higher*.'

Long may he continue to hit his critics for six.

Life of Brian

These days you really can use such phrases as 'quiet stealth' about him. During the 1983–84 season Brian Clough once again dismantled a team – and built a brand new one. And again the people's cry goes up for him to run the English national team.

He will be fifty next year and middle-age seems to have muffled his tin drum. He now reserves most of his jibes, sideswipes, and opinions for Radio Trent or the Nottingham *Evening Post*. Though his players, daily and sometimes hourly, still cringe on the end of those nasal, knowing, knocking whines, they should worry, for once again this engaging original has picked and paired, mixed and matched, his latest Nottingham Forest XI from a choice of trusty old hands, schoolboys he has nursed for years, and unconsidered triflers from the public parks.

This time he has done it by himself. For years his partner and buddy in management was Peter Taylor. They were, in the Nottingham legend, as together and trippingly off the tongue as Robin and Marion, Larwood and Voce, Lawton and Sewell – or, to be sure, Torvill and Dean. A year or so ago, Clough and Taylor fell out. The divorce was wrangling, then bitter, and now crackles only with fuming silences. Taylor, it was said, found and picked their teams, and Clough had only to gee them up. That myth has finally been disproved.

Taylor went up the road to Derby County, and left when they belly-flopped into the Third Division.

On their way to work each morning, the two old friends were said to pass each other on the A52 – both glowering, and with not even a headlight wink to stir remembrance.

It was at Derby County that the partnership first seeped into the consciousness of the British sporting public. In the late 1960s, the side was again in danger of sliding out of the Second Division. Inside a couple of years, Clough and Taylor took them to the First Division Championship. But they had been together far longer than that.

They met in Middlesbrough, some thirty years ago. Taylor, who is six years older, had been transferred from Coventry to be Middlesbrough's first team goalkeeper – and immediately appreciated that a raw, roustabout, reserve centre-forward who had just finished his National Service was making his gloved hands sting something terrible during practice. Aye, aye, thought Taylor, who is this nut? He is probably still thinking the same thing. Taylor became the young man's champion, persuading him and the rest of the club that he had a future. Every other day, Clough would ask for a transfer; every *other* day Taylor would talk him out of it.

When the boy finally bagged the first team's red No. 9 shirt he went gloriously bonkers and in Middlesbrough's next 271 games young Clough scored 251 goals. Nobody in League history had been quicker to 200 goals (219 games), and only the average of the legendary Dixie Dean – 283 in 300 – kept him out of the all-time record book. He played twice for England – between the two prodigies, Greaves and Charlton. Then, in 1962, in a game at Bury, his knee buckled, and that, to all intents, was that. At the age of twenty-six, he was just an unqualified, has-been footballer.

Brian once told me he had cried for a day when he realized he would never play football again. He would also cry as a kid when he saw his father, Joe, toss his Friday paypacket pittance on the kitchen table to his mother after his gruelling long week in a Middlesbrough sweet factory. Clough was one of nine children. He also cried when he failed the 11-plus.

He left Sec. Mod. at fifteen, to serve a term as office boy to a local firm. Then he was post boy and junior clerk in the local

ICI work-study department. He kicked footballs during every spare minute (opening bat in the summers), and by the time National Service began, Middlesbrough FC had at least learned to spell his name. He might even have gone back to ICI on his demob. As a reserve, the football club paid him only eleven pounds a fortnight – which all went to his mother – and the chemical firm were paying nearly double that for labourers. Then, in the golden years when he was averaging forty goals a season for the First XI, he took home seventeen pounds a week.

It was even less when he took up management after his injury. He knew he had to start at the bottom. He did. He had done some coaching at a school in Redcar (one pound four shillings an hour), and briefly looked after the Sunderland youth team. Of the ninety-two League clubs then, at the very bottom of the Fourth Division was, wouldn't you know, Hartlepool United (still, as ever, bless them, praying for survival, let alone simply re-election). Clough became the League's youngest manager in 1965.

Hartlepool's local journalists felt silly (and probably still do) when some Saturdays they had to telephone the gate receipts to the Press agencies, not in pounds but in shillings. Hartlepool was the very fount of the joky old telephone query: 'Hello, what time's kick-off?' 'When can you get here, lad?'

They had just sold their Victoria Ground to the local council, so there was no security nor room to manoeuvre with the bank. Barclays brooded. Clough withdrew his own salary. He sacked the groundsman and marked up the pitch himself. He dismissed the team's bus driver and drove the coach himself to away matches. Bells ringing for the first time, he went cap-in-hand to pubs and clubs, to the Rotary and to Darby and Joan. He raised almost £10,000 and kept the club solvent – and even managed to keep a bit back, to persuade the forgotten manager of faraway, non-League Burton Albion to become his assistant. He was Peter Taylor, one time Middlesbrough goalie.

At the end of the 1967 season, Hartlepool won promotion for the only time in their history – but by then Clough and Taylor had moved off to transform Derby County . . . and, later and spectacularly, to do the same for Nottingham Forest.

Now, on his own, Brian Clough is still at it.

Glinting Grandeur

Have you ever seen a beanpole slouching? A bespectacled beanpole, come to that, and one with gammy knees, overlong arms, and with the bewildered, almost vacant, look of Paddington Bear. Well, that was Clive Lloyd, who captained the West Indian cricket team against England for the last time this summer. He has recently celebrated his fortieth birthday.

The long, languid West Indian has been, as Jimmy Cannon said of Joe Louis, 'a credit to his race – the human race'. He can also bat a bit: indeed, like a dream; or, in the case of once glittery, now perspiring, trundlers, like a nightmare. His erstwhile county colleague at Lancashire, Peter Lever, once said, 'He doesn't accumulate runs, he *butchers* them.' As the essayist, Robertson-Glasgow, wrote of the most legendary of Lloyd's predecessors, George Headley: 'Great batting often has the beauty of the blast or the grandeur of the gale. When he walks down the pavilion steps you expect, in hope or fear.' Only three or four can do this for you always. Lloyd is one of them.

A skimming tally off the top of my head lists fifteen England cricket captains in the last twenty-one years – Dexter, Smith, Cowdrey, Close, Illingworth, Denness, Lewis, Greig, Brearley, Botham, Fletcher, Willis, Gower and, briefly, Graveney and Boycott. In that time the West Indians have had but *four* – Worrell, Sobers, Kanhai and Lloyd. Continuity and quality. They have also won just about everything in sight. Lloyd has led in their last sixty-four Tests, in which they have won twenty-eight times, a remarkably high proportion. They have lost only one of the last thirty-two Tests under his command.

By general agreement, one of the few classics of sporting literature is *Beyond a Boundary*, C. L. R. James' philosophical ramble around the Caribbean which took as its text, 'What do they know of cricket who only cricket know?' It was first published in 1963, and on re-reading it you realize its prime purpose was as a venomously trenchant pamphlet demanding that a black man be allowed to captain his national side at its national game. For until Worrell *only a man with a light skin had been allowed to captain the West Indies at cricket.*

Wrote James: 'The discrimination against black men was now an international scandal. I was primed for action and made up my mind to clean up this captaincy mess once and for all. When the MCC tour drew near I gave notice that I proposed an all-out campaign for Worrell to replace Alexander as captain.' Alexander was a white man and a Cambridge blue. James said, 'There is not the slightest shadow of justification for Alexander to be captain of a side in which Worrell was playing,' and went on to explain that 'the manipulators planned to continue sending to populations of white people (in Australia and England) black or brown men under a white captain'.

He continued. 'The more brilliantly the black men played, the more it would emphasize to millions of English people: "Yes, they are fine players, but, funny isn't it, they cannot be responsible for themselves – they must always have a white man to lead them."'

Worrell became captain, and was knighted by the Queen. The West Indian team began to be invincible, and continued to be when Sobers succeeded Worrell. He, too, was knighted.

Alexander, the white man, had still been captain when, in 1958, a long youthful gangle of limbs and specs had skipped school in Georgetown and shinned up that gum tree near the sightscreen at the evocative old Bourda ground to watch his first Test match. Sobers made a century in each innings against Pakistan and the treetopped, squinting, glinting, barefoot bag of bones was entranced.

Clive had not long worn spectacles. The year before, when he was twelve he had been walking home from the Foundation School at teatime when he saw two younger boys engaged in a furious fist fight. Even then the mediator, he stepped in to part them. The combatants were not pleased. One took a ruler from his satchel and poked Clive in the eye. He took no notice, although it was painful, but within a week he was unable to read either the blackboard in the classroom or the scoreboard at cricket. An order was put in for what was to become the most famous pair of spectacles in cricket.

He had almost given up the game in the year after the injury. The ball kept missing his bat and hitting his legs when the laddoes from Crown Street pitched their evening wicket in the Lloyds' back yard. Even more so when, in the next year, his father Arthur, chauffeur to a white doctor, had died, and the breadwinning onus fell on Clive. He became a clerk at the Georgetown Hospital, on sixteen pounds a month.

Yet he continued to be inspired at cricket by his elder cousin, Lance Gibbs, a prancing, straight-backed, classical spin bowler who was to become the Caribbean's finest. Lance gave Clive his first grown-up bat – signed by Len Hutton. And his second – signed by Everton Weekes.

Lance lent him his boots for his first match, at fifteen, for the local Demerara club. They were far too big for him. He made 12, as he did when he won his cap for Guyana against Jamaica in 1964. Four years later he played his first Test innings against England, at the Queen's Park Oval in Port-of-Spain. The English Press party had not seen him before. Some of them burst into laughter as the long streak of seeming diffidence gangled out, his pads un-blancoed, his spectacles reinforced at each ear with a twirl of Sellotape, his bat a shade of weathered mahogany and bandaged in Elastoplast.

Myopically he peered down the pitch to ask the umpire for guard. Then he hunched over the old brown bat as if the handle began somewhere around his shins. Which it did. The English players hadn't seen him before either. Some of them looked at each other and started giggling.

The mirth did not last long. England's attack, led by Snow, Brown, Lock and Titmus, was respectable, even hostile, certainly experienced. Within minutes, it was as if they were in collusion with the great, prowling, predatory, black cat – and doling him up prearranged deliveries to prove the whole show had been laid on just to exhibit the art of murderous left-handed batsmanship. He simply cudgelled them to all

47

points. He made 118 – and again, with an assassin's minimum bluster, he hit another century in the next Test in Barbados.

He has been feeding off the white men in the years since. But the pageant will soon be over. He may take his team to Australia in the winter; he may even play one more summer for his beloved, adoptive Lancashire. But from England's centre stage, the great, slouching, bear of a beanpole has languidly taken his leave.

Queue to see, for one last time, the glint of the glasses and the grandeur of the gale. Like the man said: – 'When he walks down the pavilion steps you expect, in hope or fear.' And much affection.

Green and Pleasant

It was an unlikely happening. At the anniversary celebrations of the *International Football Book*, the annual sword of honour award was given to a journalist for the first time. I don't quite know how highly this gleaming Gillette job actually rates in the worldwide game, but it's certainly higher than Bell's bottle of the month for managers, for previous winners down the years have included such administrative giants as Busby, Meisl and Rous, and players of such celestial calibre as Matthews, Pele, Charlton and Di Stefano.

The new winner is that most deservedly hallowed of hacks, Geoffrey Green, who retired some half-a-dozen years ago as football writer of *The Times*. The old boy limped up to receive his sword – and in dingy, sing-song bars around the world they raised their glasses and smiled.

In his prime, a couple of decades and more ago, Green's romance and grace and flavours began to illuminate the hitherto pragmatic, dowdy, workaday, Fleet Street styles. Down there on the green, as the whites played the reds played the blues played the yellow-away-strips, Geoffrey began to lard the whole lot in purple.

Cardus unquestionably pioneered modern cricket writing and opened the doors for a whole stream of notable successors. Golf has had Darwin, Longhurst, Ward-Thomas, Ryde and Dobereiner; boxing has had Whiting and Wilson, and still relishes Batt and McIlvanney; rubgy union's had its Toft, and so on. Soccer, thanks to Green, now has its Laceys and Glanvilles and Millers and Moynihans; out of their different stables, they would all nod acknowledgement to Geoffrey. He opened the door and let the sunshine in.

Actually, he also let in the stars and the moons and the rainbows and the windmills. And the fun and the laughter. I daresay he never split an infinitive, but by golly! he would mix the metaphors into a glorious, heady, purply brew. Then he'd finish dictating, have a large slug or two of the amber liquid and, if the match had been an especially good one, would get out his mouth organ and play 'Moon River' on the back seat of the bus all the way home. Or perhaps his beloved Satchmo's 'It's a Wonderful World'.

The Hungarians in 1953 didn't just beat England, they used 'winking, flashing lights all over Wembley, every move like a flare going through a prism'. Bobby Charlton wasn't just an excitingly fluent player in the No. 9 shirt, he was 'the dashing leader of the line on a white charger, releasing rockets from the edge of the area that go home like a clap of thunder and lift the opposing net as if a gale had struck it'.

A goalkeeper wouldn't just have an 'off' day against, say, Charlton – he would be 'all flailing arms and shut eyes, a blind windmill caught in a high gale'. Greaves was not just a sharp goal-scorer, he was 'the floppy-trousered pickpocket of the penalty area', and Finney never just ran, but 'glided like a skimming yacht on a lovely day'. Quality teams wouldn't coast to victory, they would resemble 'an errand boy free-wheeling downhill with his feet on the handlebars, whistling'. And on and on . . .

Insurance salesmen are not meant to stir in their metaphors like that. Green used to be one. After Shrewsbury and Cambridge (a 1929 blue as a tall and top-hole centre-half), he languidly ambled into adulthood – and, of course, had the statutory spell teaching at a private school ('so private that it cost about 6,000 quid a day'). He was divinity master, but a less than interested instructor to such extent that at examination time he had to give his boys the answers beforehand. He was summoned to the Headmaster. 'You're a modern Moses,' said the Head in awe, 'the lowest mark in your class is 94 per cent!' Moses basked in glory for a night, drank to his divine genius, confessed next morning, resigned, and became an insurance salesman.

Head office was in Oxford Circus. Every day he would collect his list of possible clients and trudge off to the suburbs. In six months he had not sold a penny piece. It was now the summer of 1938, June 24 to be exact. He was setting off for Surrey at nine. Hang on a mo, that bus goes to Sutton, but this one goes to Lord's. The second Test was starting that day. Insurance be damned! He was last in before they closed the gates.

He perched high on the Nursery balcony. On a dew-kissed, sprightly pitch, McCormick of Australia at once shivered the timbers of the chancer, Barnett, and the two pale nippers, Hutton and Edrich: 30 for three. At high noon, in rolled the mighty Hammond, 'a full-rigged galleon'. At close of play on a golden day, England were 409 for five, Hammond 210 not out, Paynter 99, Ames 50. Young Green never went back to the office. Ever. He's still got, somewhere, that list of possible clients for June 24, 1938.

So the last of the bums' trades just had to be beckoning. Getting in was the knack. An attractive, older, lady friend of the family, it came to pass, was being courted with heavy earnestness by a sub-editor on the racing table of *The Times*. The fellow was so much in love that he might be persuaded to do something serious. The plan was for the unemployed, lank Green, innocently and 'accidentally' to make up a four at tennis: at convenient moment over the Robinson's Barley Water, girlfriend would casually drop the drift of young Geoffrey's ambition. It worked. Certain that it would enhance the cut of the suit he was so devoutly pressing, our racing friend had an impassioned word with the boss – and in no time Green was a trainee sub on *The Times*.

And very few moons and rainbows had passed before he was standing on his first touchline duckboard: 1,000 words on the Bradfield versus Shrewsbury school match. . . .

Forty-five years and a billion words later, The Sword dips once more to The Pen.

Saint Geoffrey

Geoffrey Boycott has always been a keen letter-writer. In his twirly-youthful, ballpoint longhand, he has always been prompt, meticulous and businesslike. To me, anyway, he will always sign-off differently and jokingly. This one ended '. . . All the best – Your old Fruit 'n Nut Montgomery'.

Once, years before, I had dubbed him in print as 'old Fruit and Nut' after sitting next to him on a Guyana-bound aeroplane during which time he had consumed, solo, two of the largest bars of Cadbury's I had ever seen. 'Aye, good for energy is chocolate.' The name 'Monty' also stuck for a bit, suggested by his habit in faraway, foreign, deserty places of seldom socializing with his fellows after play and retiring to the 'caravan' of his hotel room, ordering a healthily frugal and lonely room-service, reading, writing letters, sipping ginseng tea, plotting his campaign for the morrow and, at early lights-out, dreaming his recurring dreams of 'roons and more roons'.

The nickname that stuck most readily through his career in the England dressing-room was 'Fiery', an ironic, grudging testament to his monumental, patient and diligent concentration at the crease for England.

But can any one man, in any walk of life, have so split an English county as Geoffrey Boycott has split Yorkshire?

Town Halls have been packed to the rafters in his support. Other Town Halls have been filled to castigate him. One eruption was in 1978 when they dismissed him as captain. On that occasion the *Guardian* sports pages organized an 'Ode to Sir Geoffrey' poetry competition. Hundreds entered. Some were unprintably venomous. Others were too droolingly adoring. Few were simply good fun. The winner was a Mr D. Cleaver, of Oldham, who twigged the ridiculous solemnity of the hoo-ha as well as the high-grade humour:

'Twas evenin' time in t'Vatican and t'Pope 'ad gone to bed.
'E were laid there readin' *Newsweek* wi' 'is skullcap on 'is 'ead.
At around about ten-thirty a knock came at front door
An' there stood a tiny errand boy all breathless an' footsore.
'E stood there, eyes all wet wi' tears, 'is voice about t'crack,
'Tha'd best raise t'gaffer right away – Geoff Boycott's got the
    sack!'

We recalled that verse with laughter, when Geoffrey and I had supper recently, though I must admit there was just a gleam, a passing glow from his Coventry-blue-tinted contact lenses, that wanted to agree, earnestly, that the poet had a point. If Boycott was a Catholic, some part of him would be looking already for, well if not quite a canonization yet, at least a beatification to be going on with.

We dined in a posh, sweet-trolley, ice-bucket, provincial Trust House hotel restaurant with menus like Town Criers' scrolls and waiters like unctuous *gendarmes*. No, Geoffrey didn't want any wine, only some hot water for his ginseng teabag and a bottle of mineral water. Perrier? No, certainly not Perrier, go out and get some Ashbourne water – 'I'm English, aren't I. Support home industries, that's me.' They went out to find some Ashbourne water. He didn't bother with the menu – 'I just want an 'unk of that *Dutch* cheese!' You never quite know where you are with Geoffrey.

Nobody has ever known. Except perhaps his beloved mother, the widow of an always coughing-sick miner who was latterly badly injured in an underground accident. His mother died just two weeks before he was sacked as Yorkshire's captain in 1978. 'That was the worst month of my life.'

I nudged him to remember what was surely the best day of his life – when he had walked serenely through the milling throng, moist-eyed, and sheepish grin more skew-whiff than ever, in the starling-shrieking, jabbering cockpit of that tumbledown stadium at Delhi on Christmas Eve in 1981. Five minutes before, Boycott had meticulously tucked the slow left-armer, Doshi of India, to the midwicket fence to become the most prolific batsman in the whole long, grand, history of all Test Match cricket.

This complicated, self-absorbed, warrior-hero-friend had now scored more runs under pressure than the founding-father, W.G.; more by far than the Doctor's sparkling apprentices like Jessop or Trumper or Fry or Macarteney; more than 'the Master' called Hobbs; more than the twinkle-toed, narrow-eyed bully-boy of bowling, Bowral's Bradman; more than the languid, liquid-moving, laughing cavalier called Sobers; more than the mighty Hammond, the debonair Compton, the accumulating Hanif, the three wondrous Ws; more than May or Cowdrey . . . more, many more, than predecessors in his same rosed-blue cap, the smarm-haired, ever-sound Sutcliffe and the un-racy rationalist of batting, Hutton. (Boycott's all-time hero, oddly, had never been either of those latter two fellow Tykes: when he was getting his eight O-levels at Hemsworth Grammar School, the great and graceful Wessex whiffer, Graveney, was, to the squinting, lonely mother's boy, the *nonpareil*.)

For the next two days in Delhi, Geoffrey was on a high. In public he was modesty itself, insisting that his hundredth hundred at Headingley meant more to him. But the dreamy, faraway mists would not leave his eye. On Christmas Day he was a hit at the fancy dress party in which the theme was 'Heroes'. Boycott went as Prince Ranjit-sinjhi. (Ian Botham went as Sir Geoffrey Gandhi, but that's another story!)

Then, calamitously for the new champion, a gruesomely depressing reaction settled on his mind and spirit. We moved on for the next Test in Calcutta. Geoffrey closeted himself in his room for a week. He finished the massive novel *Shogun*, but mostly had his face turned to the wall. He complained of 'utter listlessness', cried off in the middle of the Test and flew home where, 'with the whole world turned against me', he organized the rebel tour to South Africa.

My theory was that, having become statistically the most

successful batsman in history, his very driving motor simply conked out. His unlikely – impossible – ambition of thirty years had been achieved (his later, refound, greed for Yorkshire runs was to show Illingworth which of them was indispensible), and there was nothing left.

It was well over a quarter of a century before that a ludicrous – indeed laughable, on the few occasions he divulged it – determination had gripped the lonely little lad with bad eyesight who was fed up with being teased in the playground. He was going to be the best bat in the world. And so, once he had passed his 11-plus, for night upon night after school, through springs and autumns and the slush of winters, he would make two changes on the bus to travel from the family's tiny Coal Board house at 45 Milton Terrace, Fitzwilliam, to Johnny Lawrence's indoor cricket hut some twenty miles away. When he could, his cricket-loving uncle would accompany him. But the dream was Geoffrey's. 'They can laugh now. They won't when I'm the best there's ever been.'

His first, grown-up, senior League game was for Hemsworth in 1954 when he was thirteen. He went in No. 9 against Knaresborough, who had been bowled out for 119. Hemsworth had struggled to 85 for seven when the boy marched in – in spectacles, short trousers and cumbersome pads. At 118 for seven he put his left foot down the wicket and coldly drove the winning boundary . . . and his dreams that night again determined him in his course.

His nightly bus journeys continued. One Sunday, in his late teens, he was batting again for the local club, relentlessly moving towards another century. Play was interrupted with a message for him to report next day to Headingley to attend the Yorkshire first-team nets. He left the field at once, pursued by the opposition captain.

'Is it not courtesy to ask permission to leave the field in the middle of an innings?'

Boycott fixed him with a withering glare. 'I've finished with your class of cricket,' he sneered. And he went on his way.

Half a dozen years later he was walking out with Dennis Amiss to open the batting for England. 'Good luck,' said Dennis as they went to their respective ends. 'It's not luck,' snorted Geoffrey, 'it's skill.'

On another occasion, on a perfect Test wicket, Amiss accidentally ran out his partner early on. Boycott came back seething. When, an hour later, the rest of the England players on the balcony applauded Amiss' half century, a distraught Geoffrey shouted above them, 'They're *my* roons, y'clappin', *my* roons!'

In India, at one of the interminable official functions that must be attended, the small talk, of a sudden, was turned off dramatically. The gathering froze. H. M. Bateman could hardly have bettered the tableau. A diminutive Indian banker, mingling enthusiastically till then, had had the temerity to ask one of the England tourists, 'And what, good sir, is your name, may I ask?'

The famous, wonky grin sought to cut through the horrified silence. The blue eyes rolled and blazed. The little banker wobbled. Finally, one of the greatest of living Englishmen spluttered a reply in his Yorkshire accent: 'W. G. Grace! What's yours?'

We all laughed, but Geoffrey wasn't done – 'And what's more, unless I'm crackers or something, I've scored a bloody sight more roons than that bearded old bugger, too, I'm telling you!'

Football Crazy

In English international soccer, Robson has been particularly blessed with Robson. The manager, Bobby, has come across an outstanding captain in the making in Bryan Robson, an impressive young man with a verve on the field to match his charm and civility off it. A soccer captain, of course, needs few of the tactical or diplomatic credentials expected of a skipper at cricket; he has no official say in picking the team, does not have to stay up all night working out his field placings, and plays little if any part in deployment of tactics once the whistle goes. At the eye of the storm he is expected to say no more than 'Get stuck in lads!' Once it is over, 'The lads was great!' or 'We've still gotta lotta work t'do, Barry,' will suffice for public relations.

Nevertheless, English teams have been well served by captains in recent years. Bobby Moore was a credit to the game and his times, a superb positional reader of the play and an unflurried and calming influence; he was not at all fast but his schemes were born of one of the most nimble, suspicious brains ever applied to English soccer. Things were always pretty satisfactory, safe and sound when Bob was at the back. Pele always considered him the most sure – as well as the fairest – who ever marked him.

Emlyn Hughes was a different kettle as captain. He was an exuberant rallying post; he was, as they say, one-footed, and he had all the positional certainties of a pinball yet, lights flashing and buzzers buzzing, he would hare about all over the place to make amends; his voice was pitched almost as highly as Alan Ball's and his 'Get stuck in!' was an imploring screech of both daring and desperation; they called him 'Horse' as in Crazy Horse and in his day he led some fair old hollering charges. In the same mould was Kevin Keegan, another limited player and lucky to shine in mediocre times; he was a curly-coiffed toy terrier, barking and snapping and always looking to give 101 per cent; the pack followed him readily and faithfully and without question – and in and out of many a cul-de-sac. For a time it seemed *he* was English International soccer.

Bobby Robson's first decision as England's manager was to drop Keegan. The player briefly spat and spluttered and acted like a spoiled baby, then 'retired' to the Second Division. Robson ignored the outburst; he knew he had someone else, with the promise of far more potency, around which to build his team. Bryan Robson took to the

centre-stage. He has what they call vision; he has 'two feet'; he tackles fairly, but with all the clean-cut certainty of a pair of new pruning shears; he times his runs into challenging positions with a surprise and crescendo which can be thrilling. In turn he is aggressive and calming, observant, creative and industrious. He leads by example and consideration, stealth as well as exhortation. Bryan Robson is extremely good news.

Like all born leaders, young Robson can separate pride from vanity. Though, of course, he gets a small fortune in his little brown envelope each Friday, there seems more than a touch of the Corinthian spirit about Robson. Through his workrate shines the hint of the amateur.

Mind you, a century ago he *would* have been an amateur. In 1884, England selected a professional to play for the first time – Forrest, J. H., of Blackburn Rovers. Their opponents, Scotland, objected, only relenting when the English announced that he would wear a different coloured shirt from the rest of their side. The following year, when Gents mixed with players on the field, the Football Association still insisted on different shirts, and as *Athletic News* pointed out on 5 November that year, 'the dark blue shirts savoured of the collier . . . and the Gentlemen were clad in spotless whites.'

Nine years later, an international trial was arranged at Nottingham – Gents versus Players. The professionals won by 9–0, and ten of them were selected for the national side – with the one amateur, of course, as captain. Indeed, as the comparatively radical *Athletic News* observed: 'We have very little doubt that well-behaved pros would have found their captain a very sociable captain had he given them a chance.' The paper went on to complain that the skipper travelled first-class on the train 'and yet did not recognize his men, nor speak to them in any way, left them severely alone in driving to the match, and generally behaved as if he was a superior sort of being.'

England's first professional captain was Robert Crompton of Blackburn in the first international match of this century. Since when, for 'Play Up, Chaps!' read 'Get Stuck In, Lads!'

Three Score and Ten

John Arlott celebrated his seventieth birthday recently. Around noon on the day – or perhaps just a touch before – he selected something special from the cellar of his Alderney home (called, wouldn't you know, 'The Vines'). He had a momentary sniff as the glass reached his lips. He took a sip, then, at once, a much longer one. An almost imperceptible, reverent, nod; a teeny twitch of a smile, and the soft-boiled, old spaniel eyes glinted in equal measures of satisfaction and melancholy at his seventy years before the mast.

The eyes moistened more, and the great spotted handkerchief unfurled to dab an eye, to mop the brow, to have a mighty blow. Then another swig. Then, perhaps, a joke to help start the day. Usually a shaggy-dog tail-wagger. Stop me if you've heard it. You very seldom have. And anyway, with John Arlott more than anyone, it-ain't-what-y'say-it's-the-way-that-y'say-it.

Actually, that's not true. It was also *what* he said. As one of history's grandest radio broadcasters, he was up there on the plinth alongside Murrow and Dimbleby and Cooke.

'This of a cloudy Lord's morning . . . and Lillee's balding head turns – lightly tonsured you might say – and he moves away from us, chasing his shadow . . . the pigeons like vultures for him . . . and Boycott has gone, his helmet now off and in the crook of his arm, like a Knight at Arms, "alone and palely loitering".'

That sort of thing . . . and when you read the words, you hear, gruffly loud, the yeoman's voice of Wessex.

Three score and ten. It means he was thirty-three when

those rich, thick-soupy vowels first stirred the consciousness of this eight-year-old. If I had the reference books I could look the details up precisely. It was Trent Bridge, 1947, England v South Africa. Who was bowling? Was it Martin of Kent? Or Butler of Notts? Anyway, the voice said, 'And he turns and moves in,' and then he counted the bowler's paces, 'one, two, three, four, five, six, seven . . . over she goes . . . and . . . *he's bowled him!*' I was hooked.

I can also give you, pretty well verbatim I think, his commentary at the Oval in the following year when Don Bradman played his final Test innings. The bowler was Eric Hollies, a cheerily rotund leg spinner from Warwick. When Bradman arrived at the wicket, the England captain, Norman Yardley, had led the England team, caps aloft, in three hurrahs. And then: '. . . It's Hollies then from the Vauxhall end. He bowls. Bradman goes back across his wicket and pushes the ball gently towards the direction of the Houses of Parliament out there beyond mid-off. It doesn't go that far, of course, but merely to Watkins at silly mid-off. No run. Two slips and a forward short-leg. Hollies again. He pitches the ball slowly up to him. *And he's bowled!* Bradman . . . bowled Hollies . . . nought. Well, what can you say in such circumstances? I wonder if you see a ball very clearly in your last Test in England, on a ground where you have played out some of the biggest cricket of your life, and when the opposing team have just given you three cheers . . . Indeed I wonder if you really see the ball at all. . . .?'

The voice was slightly sharper then, more tangy. For the next thirty-two years it weathered and mellowed into a national institution. It signed off, appropriately on the last day of the Centenary Test in 1980. I have the recording: '. . . And Boycott pushes this away between silly-point and slip, picked up by Mallett at short third man; that's the end of the over; it's 69 for two, nine runs off the over, 28 Boycott, 15 Gower, 69 for two, and after Trevor Bailey it'll be Christopher Martin-Jenkins . . .'

Just like that. No frills, no fuss. I was standing behind him in 'the box' that day. Finished, he took a large swig of claret. Then mopped his brow with the great spotted hankie, and prepared to leave for ever.

Then something astonishing happened. The Lord's public address announced that John had finished his final broadcast at a Test match. The whole ground spontaneously applauded. Boycott put down his bat to clap. All the players joined in. Lillee, even, stopped in his tracks to turn and wave a fisted salute towards the commentators' eyrie high on the pavilion turret.

And the embarrassed object of everyone's affection took another large gulp from his glass, and hurried away.

He sold his house in Hampshire and much of his wine and many of his books. He retired to Alderney – to enjoy three-quarters of the hobbies he lists in *Who's Who*: 'drinking wine, talking, sleeping'. The other one – 'watching cricket' – he has given up. Alas.

Paisley Pattern

If you catch him in a suit it's a John Collier 'budget buy' off the peg. He does admit to a weakness for gaudy neckties; usually they clash with a battered, old, lived-in tent of a soft brown sports jacket which effortlessly contains the amply rotund figure. Sometimes it's an unsnazzy, crumpled tracksuit, though Bob Paisley, now retired from the game, was not what you would really call a tracksuit manager.

What's left of his hair is slicked down with Brilliantine. The eyes are sharp and kestrel-bright still, which is understandable for this elderly man is, statistically, the most successful manager of a Football League side in all the long history of the English professional game. In less than ten years under his guidance, Liverpool won an astonishing five League Championships, five titles in Europe, and two League Cups.

In a tiresome television age in which bangled, beaded, coiffed and zoot-suited First Division managers are expected to squawk with the tiresome banality of a cop car siren at the drop of a point, Paisley is the most unlikely of heavy weight champions. He is what he is; he looks what he is: that battered, lived-in sports jacket matches his battered, lived-in, hale and purply face. You would be right to mistake him for a pensioner whose main hobby, other than studying racehorse form, was dandling grandchildren on his knee; a working man from the Durham minefields, an elementary schoolboy from the Depression of half a century ago where the thing to do was play street football, keep pigeons and train whippets – and then go off to the desert at Monty's call to the colours and kick sand in the face of Rommel. When he returned from the war he was a grisly, strong, combative wing-half and he joined Liverpool FC. His team mates called him 'The Rat', as in desert.

He won a League Championship medal in 1947, but was left out of the FA Cup Final against Arsenal after scoring in the semi-final. When he retired as a player he stayed on at Anfield, backroom boy in the bootroom, bringing up the rear as trainer, coach, confessor and sar'nt major i/c the sponge and the skip.

Over twenty years ago, Bill Shankly, an extrovert Scot who had also been a miner and a wing-half, arrived to manage Liverpool. He had an involved and involving innocence and a passionate feel for football and footballers. Everton were the plush, lush, city topcats. Shankly announced there were only two class Mersey sides – Liverpool and Liverpool Reserves. And then he set about proving it. In 1962 he brought them out of the Second Division and thereafter – and in time to the blossoming pop music renaissance in the city – Shankly's Liverpool formed a brand new fringe culture of their own.

As Arthur Hopcraft observed at the time in his evocative book, *The Football Man*: 'We have a plainsong of the terraces. It was created in Liverpool where the city character, with its pervading harshness of waterfront life and bitterly combative Irish exile content was given a sudden flowering ... more than any other English city, Liverpool experiences its hope and shame through its football. Vivid memories are frozen in my mind of crowd scenes; the sight of a small ragged boy appearing gracefully on the skyline of the Kop's slanting roof, stepping gracefully down and sitting down, arms folded, a tiny symbolic representative of the bravura of his people.'

Shankly, the standard bearer, was canonized by half a city. Next to him on the bench was always Bob Paisley with the bucket and sponge. The congregation had eyes only for Shanks and his ponies, his pride and joy, his ten red devils and the goalie in green. The world fed off Shankly's wit and convoluted wisdom. He denied the story that he'd taken his wife to a reserve team match on their wedding anniversary – 'D'ye think I'd have got wed during the season!' he rasped. The doctor ordered him to take a holiday from football. He went to Blackpool for a week and returned to announce that it had been 'a wonderful break – I got up a team among the hotel guests and we beat the waiters hollow!'

He accused a journalist of inaccuracy – 'I never *drop* players, laddie: I only make changes.' When his teams were charged with being too predictable, he would sneer – 'Aye, Joe Louis was pretty predictable, too!' When supporters, at either Wembley or in Woolworths, would (honestly) kneel to kiss his shiny black shoes, he would allow it with an equal reverence, saying, 'It's not respect for me, y'see, it's respect for Liverpool.' In front of the Kop he chided a cop for screwing up a fan's scarf: 'Don't do that – it's the wee lad's very life.'

Shankly retired in 1974 and named as his successor his old unsung backroom boy. It was a hard act to follow. At first, any success for Paisley was considered to have been won simply on the back of Shankly's great foundations. Now, eight years later, some are saying that Shankly's great success was won on the back of his unsung No. 2's foundations.

Paisley had, if anything, more steely resolve and lack of sentiment than the passionate, more volatile Shankly. What he was seen to do, which the more emotional Shankly sometimes dithered over, was break up a team when it was *still* winning and when, to the unpractised eye, everything seemed hunky-dory. His transfusions of new blood were regular yet almost imperceptible. In eight years he dismantled and built three new teams.

I remember Paisley on the night of what he considers still to be his greatest triumph, Rome, 1977, when Liverpool won their first European Cup. At the Holiday Inn, the champagne flowed, Emlyn, Kevin, Tommy, Ray, Bollinger and Co. were uncorking satisfaction, high spirits and fizz. A plump man with a purply face and a crumply suit tugged conspiratorially at my sleeve. 'You wouldn't know, son,' he asked, 'if you can lay your hands on a Guinness in this place?'

Both feet on the ground. Like the time one of his newer first-team players made an appointment to ask for a rise. The boy did so, adding for impressive good measure, that the club hadn't yet seen the best of him on the field. Paisley deflated the aspirant with the whispered throwaway – 'Well, thank goodness for that, son.'

Paisley's was the hardest act of all to follow.

But Joe Fagan did it.

Batting for Britain

I, for one, missed Bob Willis when the world and his wife decided he had captained the England cricket team for the last time. However button-eyed and puppet-like he came over in his post-match TV interviews, he was much loved by his side and, on the field, his chivalries were exemplary. He bowled his boots off, but would always come out of his trance to honour the foe. International cricket needed a dose of Willis.

Nevertheless, we must all have had our spines riddled with a little *frisson* at the news of David Gower taking over. It's not too often that teenage Golden Wonders are still glinting ten years later. This is a twenty-four carat job. He can bat a bit too.

When Willis came home early from the Pakistan tour, ill, and intent to see his new baby daughter for the first time he managed the tightest lipped 'No comment' since Job. When Gower got back, he told the *Daily Star* with carefree, shrugging, charm: 'Okay, are we all supposed to be teetotal monks? Cricketers are social animals, we like to meet people and have a few drinks at the end of play. On tour there's no way we would survive otherwise; we'd go potty.' Okay, next question?

You would expect no less from Gower.

This engaging young man enjoys music, travel and wines. He was on *Desert Island Discs* and found choosing eight from thousands more taxing than facing Roberts, Holding, Garner and Marshall for eight hours in Jamaica. In the end he chose

Handel, Elton John, Genesis, Beethoven, Supertramp, Dire Straights, Al Stewart and Vaughan Williams. His island luxury was an unending supply of *Rumpole of the Bailey* video tapes, and he would also like, please, the world's very best *Dictionary of Wines*. Even if it's in French. No mention of *Wisden*.

His grandmother and mother were the musicians. Mother was also a fine tennis player. Dad was the all-round sportsman. He was in the Colonial Service, based mostly in Rhodesia. The boy was sent to King's School, Canterbury: three A- and eight O-levels later he was up at London University reading for a degree in law.

The family had settled by this time in Loughborough. A day or two after moping through his first year exams – 'suppose I would have been a country solicitor' – he answered an SOS to play for Leicestershire at Worcester. University

never saw him again. All future tutorials were taken by the likes of Mick Norman, Ray Illingworth and Jack Birkenshaw.

Friends who were there tell me that his two centuries against Pakistan – coinciding with his assumption to the England captaincy – were so assured that, after Richards and Gavaskar, he must now be considered the world's best batsman. But 'assurance' is not the word to associate with Gower. His art is delectable, his craft carefree. They moan even when he gets plenty, looking full of casual grace; they moan even more when he gets nothing: for his ducks, too, contrive a casual grace.

One of the loveliest, classicist's pleasures about Gower's batting is his serenity and stillness as the bowler approaches. Richards has that too, but you know *he's* thinking mayhem and murder. With Gower the fluent grandeur is more refined, more languid; it has a cultured, Edwardian stamp.

Historians with long beards liken Gower to England's long-ago left-handed ace, Woolley. We have the young man's mother to thank for that. When David was four, in the back garden in Rhodesia, his father would bowl the boy tennis ball lobs, but insist he played *right-handed* – till Mother stepped in and ordered that her curly-haired blond 'Bubbles' should play whichever way he wanted to!

I never saw Woolley, of course, but till I watched Gower saunter from the pav, I wondered what all the fuss could have been about – no left-hander can have the truly *classic* grace, I thought.

I looked up the late, loved essayist and county trundler, R. C. Robertson Glasgow, who bowled against Woolley. He might have been writing about Gower: 'The only policy was to pitch up the ball and hope. He could never properly be described as "set" since he did not go through the habitual process of becoming set. He jumped to his meridian. He might hit the first ball of the match, a good ball too if left to itself, crack to the boundary over mid-on; then, when he had made fifty or more, he might snick a short one past slip in a sudden freak of fallibility, a whim of humanity.'

So, too, with David Gower. Simply, when you think of his best innings, however short, you think of a perfect summer's day. He can bat, they say, as Woolley did, as it is sometimes shown in dreams.

Robson's Choice

On November 25, 1953, the insular, arrogant English were trounced by the Hungarians, by 6–3. It was the first time in history that England had been beaten at home. Next morning, Geoffrey Green wrote in *The Times* of Hungary's 'rich, overflowing and, to English patriots, unbelievable victory over an England side that was cut to ribbons for most of an astonishing afternoon. Here, indeed, did we attend the twilight of the gods.'

When England manager Bobby Robson settled into one of those moulded plastic bucket seats that serve as the Wembley 'bench' for the latest game against Hungary, no doubt he fixed a nostalgic, watery eye, and winked a remembrance to the very spot over there on the terraces where he stood on the day that England's ponderous WM formation withered in the face of the MM line-up. The Magyar Marvels, indeed.

Robson was a Fulham reserve then. He and his mates caught an omnibus from Craven Cottage at 11 am. They'd heard these Hungarians were pretty nifty. 'They might even give us a good game,' we were all saying. The bus went through Hammersmith and up the Harrow Road. For the scrawny Robson the route might have been marked 'Damascus Road'. They queued at the turnstiles. 'Once we were in, the Hungarians came out to warm up. Nobody in Britain had ever heard of warming up, and all around us people were thinking "this is a rum do," and they were all laughing and saying "they'll be knackered before the game." But then they kicked off and it was obvious from the very beginning that England would be thrashed.'

England, says Robson, worked in little triangles in those days, 'but the Hungarians had every player involved in the team unit. When England were ripped apart that day it had a profound effect that has never left me.' Soon afterwards he started attending FA coaching courses at Paddington Street, just off Baker Street, and gave up his part-time apprenticeship with an electrician. He was on his way. And now, thirty years on, Bobby's on the bench.

That seat under the Royal Box at England's musty, dusty, ancient 'national' stadium has become part of the legend. Remember how Alf Ramsey would hunch there, stone-faced whatever the score. 'Sit down, Shepherdson, and pull yourself together!' he muttered to his magic spongeman when Hurst scored England's whooping fourth on that golden summer's day in 1966. For Leeds and England, Don Readies, er, I mean *Revie*, stared out, tortured, from that bench for a decade. More often than not he would lose unloseable Cup finals and, for England, have to endure that exit around the greyhound track perimeter, hands deep in Gannex pockets, collar turned up as if to muffle the baying melody, 'What a load of rubbish!'

Then Uncle Ron: he had to march off in time to those anthems more than a few times. Dear old Greenwood would look permanently glum, kneading his Granny Giles lips throughout the game, then would mope off with a world-weary sigh to over-enunciate such homilies to the nation as 'bein' given chances and not takin' them, that's what life's all about, isn't it, Barry?'

Benched, Robson is more restless than his predecessors. He tries to be nonchalant, attempts in turn the carefree look, or that of the impassive tactician. Then an involuntary twitch takes a grip on the expressive, rubbery, pale face and it gives the game away. His eyes get oystery at whichever end of the emotional scale his heart may be. For most of the time he tries to sit calm – then suddenly he's not there, but up at the back chatting to a substitute or trainer. But always with a haunted, anguished glance at the patterns on the pitch.

The most triumphant concert Robson has conducted from this Wembley bench was in 1978 when his club side, Ipswich Town, laid waste the Arsenal in a beautifully paced, exuberant show in the Cup Final. That was the day the

Ipswich president, Lady Blanche Cobbold, was asked in the Royal retiring room if she'd like to meet Mrs Thatcher. 'Frankly, I'd much rather a gin and tonic,' she replied. That was also the day, after the match, that Mrs Thatcher was asked by Radio Two who she thought was Man of the Match. 'Unquestionably', she trilled, 'it was Whymark, the man in the No. 10 blue shirt!' She was probably trying to be funny. But her advisers had been too clever-clogs. The injured Whymark had pulled out on the eve of the match. Her nation chortled.

Robson's spaniel dog is called Roger – after Osborne, the boy who scored the winning goal for Ipswich that afternoon. I popped in to have a drink with England's manager at his handsome Ipswich home. It was a lovely, soft, East Anglian day. We sat on the patio and the buzz was from the birds and the bees and the sycamore trees, . . . and Robson rabbitting on about gardening. You want to get the griff on the England footballers, but here he was rhubarbing on about his vegetable patch . . . or that serene weeping-willow by the potting shed, or the chestnut, or the purply brightness of that clematis blue over there. Bright Ipswich blue.

Okay, gardening's one thing, but what about this drink, then? He comes back from the kitchen. Sorry, not even a Double Diamond. His rugby-playing sons must have polished off the last one the day before. Well, fancy that; soccer managers in England aren't meant to keep a dry fridge. They are meant to be pretty free with the fizz, the real McMoet. And, come to think of it, where were all the gold necklaces, the six-inch Havanas, the rings and the ringlets, the Gucci pumps with gold buckles? No offence to your Atkinsons, Allisons and Bonds, but 'Gerraway with you!' says Robson. His brown slip-on shoes cost just a few quid – 'this is the second year they've done me; nice, aren't they?' The most expensive suit he has ever bought cost exactly one hundred pounds – for the Cup final in 1978. Where from, Savile Row? 'Don't be daft – from Ridleys, the Ipswich outfitters.'

His only passion is football – learned in the north-east, at Langley Park, by kicking around a lump of coal all day if there wasn't a tennis ball handy. And every other Saturday his coal-mining dad would take his son the seventeen-mile journey to Newcastle – 'regular as clockwork, from the bus station we'd walk to Fenwicks for a cup of tea, then on to St James' Park. As often as not we were first in the queue.' And then his Magpies of United would sing for him . . . Wayman and Cowell, Stubbins, McMichael and Milburn!

His eyes moist up at the memory. Like when he thinks of Hungary and thirty years ago.

ON TOUR

Long Stop

The travel business was late in discovering sport. Once the pennies started dropping they more than made up for it.

Come the autumn, British club cricketers will be tweaking their off-breaks in California, Hong Kong, Malta and Corfu. Most popular is Barbados, and for several weeks the little island will be littered with hearty, white, flannelled fools, their wives bringing up the rear with the raffia basket, the suntan and the scorebook.

Touring rugger buggers get blind drunk in the South Seas, the deep West or the Far East. Tennis schools, run like concentration camps, have sprung up all over Iberia: British secretaries flock to them, looking for a man as well as an improvement in their overarm service. For oodles of *pesetas* they are usually just shouted at by hairy-legged *führers* in tracksuit tops, but return home insisting it was fab. Alongside these tennis courts, an increasing amount of lush green golf courses have been planted, on which brown-eyed urchins who look like Ballesteros will sniggeringly caddy for bunkered bores who swear in English as they blast on, full of sand and fury.

Back home, the travel agents keep the score with a smile. They also serve who only stand and stare, for there is good business to be had from the travelling spectator. Each winter many will fly – literally to the ends of the earth – to follow the England cricket team. They are a gentle lot, such cricket watchers. I have observed them unravelling their deckchairs, unscrewing the Thermos and settling down for the day to watch the cricket as though it was a Wednesday at Worcester, not a seething, scorching, Saturday alongside 85,000 raucous partisans at Eden Gardens, Calcutta.

I have often been touched by the kindness and courtesy the England players show to these awed fellow travellers. We journalists think ourselves a superior class of hangers-on and some scribblers find the 'coach party' spectators tiresome and irritating. When such tours started in earnest a few years ago, one of us, with some sort of genius, cruelly christened the holidaymakers 'Winks' – as in 'Wallies Incorporated'. The name has stuck.

I was once a Wink. Some winters ago I joined a party of cricket nuts to watch two Test Matches in Australia. Just ordinary folk – postmen, a farmer, a doctor, a railwayman, a retired insurance broker, about thirty of us – indulging in the great passion and, in almost every case, fulfilling the one-off, saved-for, lifelong ambition. To cut costs we flew from Heathrow on an Indonesian Airlines' 'stopper'. The flight took two days out of our lives. At one point it nearly ended our lives.

I sat next to a charming retired solicitor from Yorkshire. He and his grey-bunned auntie of a wife had never once been in an aircraft before. She scarcely stopped knitting throughout the journey. At Bali we attempted a night landing through a tropical storm. They were thrilled to bits as fearsome lightning lasered in on our fragile little porthole. 'Ee, luv, looka that, ain't nature wonderful?' I was cringing in fright. They, bless them and unknowing, had implicit faith and thought such was just a routine occurrence.

We were almost on the ground when suddenly (as we learned later) all the lights on the runway went out as a bolt from the electric blue hit the control tower. Our pilot went into full boost and we reared up vertically like a Garner bouncer. Now the cabin staff looked terribly scared too: a sure sign. In accelerating to full throttle the pilot (later) said that the left engine had blown.

The lightning outside strobed on like Guy Fawkes night. We circled around, a winged and wounded bird. People were being sick. Moslems were wailing; the rosaries of Christians were ticking away like time-bombs. I thanked God for a good life and hoped only that it wouldn't hurt. You could feel the pilot preparing to attempt, wonkily, a second landing approach. Here we go, I thought. Time up. Bali-Hi! And cheerio.

The only two completely unperturbed were the first-time fliers next to me. Auntie's knitting needles contentedly clacked on in time to the rosary beads. Her husband nudged me in affectionate conspiracy, and spoke:

'Frank, ol' lad, what d'you reckon? I'm none too 'appy about Taylor's "keepin'"' these last few Tests, don't y'think our David Bairstow should be given a chance w' t'gloves?'

I survived to tell the tale. But I have never Winked since. And when I went over to the other side on subsequent tours I was introduced to the heartless, yet harmless, game played by the travelling journalists. It can start as soon as the chartered flights begin landing and the first Winks emerge from England, blinking, or Winking, into the harsh sunlight.

You have to keep your wits about you. Beers are bought for the best of the day. Say an obvious old Wink in his MCC tie has a bad leg and limps into the hotel bar on a walking-stick, the winning line from the *hic* of hacks in the corner might be – 'Ooh! Look! A Wink on a stick!'

Perhaps a holidaymaker on a West Indies tour has been too enthusiastically introducing himself to the rum; the sentence of the day might be 'Look! A tiddly Wink!' Nudge, nudge, that one seems a bit camp. 'Sure, a sod is as good as a Wink!' At sunset, a couple of them might be walking, arm in arm, along the beach. We know the wife to be called Penelope (many of them are). Ah, what a perfect picture they make, someone might remark. 'More like a Pen and Wink drawing!'

Alas, the marauding hordes of hooligans have long driven away the genuine Winks from British soccer trips abroad. Not that any soccer men seem to know the difference between Home and Away. Once when the splendidly lugubrious and single-minded Gordon Lee was managing Everton, his side played a match in Tunisia.

Chartered flight from Liverpool; hotel; wash and brush-up; down to the bar for a lager.

'Well, boss,' a player greeted him, 'how d'you like Africa then?' Gordon did a momentary double-take, then sneered: 'Don't be bloody daft, lad – this isn't Africa, it's Tunisia!'

Court Circular

It lasts little more than a month. It creeps up on you, unsuspected, and suddenly it's almost midsummer . . . first that scent of pine and cedar and the marble-echoing, jabbering noise of Rome's Foro Italico; then the swirl of dust, the swish of fashion, and the po-faced pat-a-cake play of the baseliners at the Roland Garros in Paris; in next to no time London will be full of both the same Virginias and the same creeps at Virginia-creepered, purple-nosed, old Wimbledon, and it will be well past midsummer's day and a tennis year will have gone in just five or six weeks.

This side of the water, I fancy, we like to think the world's tennis players practise in private for eleven months solely for their month of public appearances in Europe. In fact, the circus has been hitting town after town, week after week, for the twelvemonth. A top player himself is both tourist and one of the sights. 'Slow courts, fast women? And ain't that the bridge Horatio kept? So this must be Rome!'

'Hey, if we're dining tonight in Castels in the Rue Princess, this must be Paris an' I'm still in the doubles!' What's *Nouvelles balles, s'il vous plaît* in Japanese or German or Serbo-Croat? In Italian it sounds something like *Boiled eggs for a favour*.

Modern tennis players are troubadours in combat. To adjust they must suspend time and place. The great and good Arthur Ashe once opined, 'We must pretend it is us who are standing still while the rest of the world is moving.' Playing the circuit is akin to sitting in a room changing TV channels. Said Ashe: 'You try to beat a man's brains out on court, take money out of his pocket, and then you return to the locker room with him, take a shower next to him, eat with him, drink with him, practise with him, chase women with him, maybe even play doubles with him; and two weeks or two months later, you draw him again, in Barcelona or Manila or Chicago, and all of a sudden you look across the net and it occurs to you that this is the same sonuvabitch who beat you in Vancouver the last time and you give him no quarter, and ignore him when you pass next to each other between games, and then you shake his hand when you beat him or he beats you, and you have a beer together and share a cab back to the hotel.'

Till the next time, where the courts will be different, like the restaurants and the money and the spectators; but the experience will be the same.

It must be said that, to many, the week's shenanigans at the Roland Garros courts through the Bois de Boulogne at the Porte d'Auteuil represent the very peak of the tennis year. Certainly there is more of a feeling that the world game has come together *socially* than at Wimbledon. The days seem more leisurely and the nights more languid and long. For the players, Wimbledon's fast grass represents more of a machine-gunner's lottery. In Paris, the clay courts make for gruelling, patient matches; games become an exacting

challenge for both muscles and mind. None of Martina's wham-bam-thank-you-ma'am in Paris.

Said the ace with the pace and the smile, Lew Hoad: 'Every year you say you'll never play Paris again. Your arm nearly falls off. The balls are heavy. They water the courts. You're always playing some guy you've never heard of and he keeps you out there for well over three and a half hours. *But it's a great tournament!'*

Roland Garros was a legendary Biggles-like French aviator in World War One. The courts were first opened in 1928 and became an immediate showcase for the four Musketeers – Cochet, Lacoste, Borotra and Brugnon – who spent their summers defending the valour of France against the likes of Tilden and Budge, Perry and Austin. Once, to put off Perry as he was about to serve, the bounding Basque, Borotra, held up the game, rummaged in his courtside bag and made great to-do about putting on his beret. Next point, Perry did the same and produced a great big sun-visored jockey's cap; common enough today, but it caused a sensation then – and Borotra went to pieces.

Perry was seventy-five last birthday. The long, lean, old warrior is still as handsome as ever, and happily recovered from a long illness. The day after his birthday he was able to attend a ceremony at Wimbledon where the Duchess of Kent unveiled a statue of him, in typical midcourt pose. Offhand, I can think of only one other sportsman being put, literally, on a pedestal at the scene of his triumphs – the dashing 'father' of Indian cricket, C. K. Nayudu, is hitting a sculptured sixer outside his home stadium at Indore. Perhaps there is a statue of Pele in Rio, or of Bradman at Sydney or Adelaide, but I cannot recall them. The gates dedicated to Grace and Hobbs at Lord's and the Oval aren't quite the same. Why not, come to think of it, a statue of Best at Old Trafford, or of Gareth and Barry at the Arms Park? Or of St Jack at St Andrews?

Perry still tells you that the greatest player he ever saw was the American, Bill Tilden. Big Bill, he reckons, would have eaten McEnroe for breakfast, and would even have drawn blood from the sombre Swedish stone, Borg.

Such ruminations had me, the other night, looking up Tilden's 1930s instructional book, *Match Play and the Spin of the*

Ball. In it the old champion lists his 'Thirteen Points for Young Players to Remember'. They strike me still as a priceless baker's dozen to be learned by everyone from this week's champion millionaire to last night's *Yours! – Sorry partner!* hacker on all the world's public parks:

1. Get the ball back.
2. The main object is to break up the other man's game.
3. Play defensively with an offensive attitude.
4. Play to your opponent's strength but go for his weakness at crucial points.
5. Double faults are inexcusable so develop a second serve as difficult as your first.
6. Returning is just as important as serving because fifty per cent of all points begin that way.
7. Never ever blow an easy shot.
8. Realize a champion will miss as many shots as a non-champion – but never at crucial moments.
9. Play hardest of all at 30–15, or 15–30.
10. Start a match with an alternative strategy up your sleeve – but never change a winning game.
11. Decide where your opponent might return the ball and head there pronto. Anticipation is just a fancy word for guessing right.
12. Results are more important than form. Vary pace of spin if your opponent thinks he is in a winning groove.
13. Have a killer instinct but also be a sportsman.

To which Arthur Ashe might perhaps add:

Drink water between games as a cure for jet lag.

Grand Tours

I admit to a twinge of jealousy when I saw the England cricket team off at Gatwick. I have had two or three recent winters touring with them. It was fun. They are good and singular fellows.

As I returned on the train from the airport to London's wintery chill I could picture them already lolling about their aircraft, changed from their blazers and regulation black shoes into track suits and loafers. Willis would be into his new, regulation, long novel: last winter it was *Brideshead Revisited*, the year before *The Collected Wodehouse*. Gower would already have rattled off the *Telegraph* crossword and would now be looking around for somebody with a *Times* or *Guardian*. He would gobble up both sets of clues in only an hour or two.

As sure as eggs, Gatting would be engrossed in a massive tome of science fiction; Dilley and Cowans, the young fast bowlers, would be plugged into their Walkman cassette players; Bob Taylor, the veteran wicketkeeper, would probably have started the first of his many letters home (he has called his house at Stoke-on-Trent, *Hambledon*, and that's where his heart is in more ways than one). Somewhere at the back of the aeroplane, the mighty Botham would be larking about with his great buddy, Lamb. That restless and lovable eccentric, Randall, would as usual be the butt of their amiably oafish jokes.

Travelling to the ends of the earth with a cricket bat is not like it used to be. Forty-eight years ago, Neville Cardus sailed

Down Under with the MCC team on the *Orion*. It took five weeks, and Cardus started writing his log: 'The team went about their pleasures. Verity read *The Seven Pillars of Wisdom* from beginning to end. Hammond won at all games, from chess to quoits. Maurice Layland smoked his pipe, and Duckworth danced each evening with a nice understanding of what, socially, he was doing. Wyatt took many photographs and developed them himself. Fry, who was covering the tour as a journalist, was armed with the most complicated of all cameras . . . and we passed little islands and all the adventure stories of our youth sprang to life, and here was Stevenson, Ballantyne, Defoe; on that little beach over there, silent and empty, there is surely Man Friday's footprint. . . .'

For England's latest tourists, the journey will not take even a day. At 'night', say after the film show, Gatting will doubtless discard his sci-fi for an hour or two and, with Gower and Tavare, will look to make up a four at bridge.

As the young athletes around them read and doze and dream amid the jetlagged scents of sweat and socks and private parts, the 'climate' will at least be bearable, sanitized, and fully air-conditioned. In 1936, the MCC manager was Captain Howard, of Lancashire. As the *Orion* chugged through the Red Sea one night, Cardus met him on the deck. . . . 'It was just before dinner; Capt. Howard had only ten minutes ago changed into his dinner jacket. His collar was already a rag; Mr Gladstone, after four hours or so of eloquence, never more drastically reduced stiff linen to this state of shapeless wetness. From the foreheads of all of us waterfalls are descending, splashing and dashing like the cascades of a Southey poem.'

In 1936, every member of the MCC side had to dress for dinner! This lot, nearly half-a-century later, would have been in shorts and T-shirts for their first supper of the tour. Like their stiff-collared predecessors, however, they will also have two unending sources of complaint over the next three months they are away – the food and the accommodation. Thus it always was and always will be.

I remember, on his last tour as assistant manager, the late and much-loved Kenny Barrington answering a young player's moans about conditions today in the West Indies.

Old Ken shook his head in exasperation and launched into a memorable sermon about the bad old days when he was a touring cricketer himself: 'I dunno, I really don't. Why, when we was in this place back in the Fifties with Peter May's lot, the cockroaches was so big that even when you'd trod on them as hard as you could, you'd lift your foot but they'd still be there, and they'd look up at you as if to say "good morning" and then they'd gently amble off into the woodwork!'

'You blokes don't know what good times are. Once I had 27 hours in a Pakistani train with only a bucket as a latrine, blimey! that was some tour that was. Five months when my total diet, honest to God, was eggs an' chips. Old Closey was my roommate, you ask him: once he was so ill for a whole week that all he could do was crawl from his bed to the loo on all fours every five minutes. That's all he did for a whole week. And that's a lot of crawling and a lot of crapping, I'm telling you. He never had another curry after that. He came onto my diet. Egg an' chips. 'Cos you can't muck around with eggs, and you can't muck around with chips, can you?'

So the new adventure starts for England's latest travellers. As they flew out to the faraway fields – amid the books and the cards and the jokes and the moans, just as it ever was – I daresay that only three of the young men were actually thinking about *cricket*. Three boys are on their first expedition. One new boy usually makes the grade. One might come back a minor celebrity. I wonder which?

How The West Won

They have selected the South-West Counties combined Rugby Union team to meet the New Zealand All Black tourists. It is chocker with Gloucester, Bristol and Bath men. Although a Gloucestershire man myself – even with allegiance strained of late by the tone and nasty temper of their play – it is criminal that they seldom find room for at least one Cornishman in the side.

In terms of results, Cornish county rugby has been set on a slack sail in recent years, but the spirit and *ethos* of the olde tyme game still beats with a gutsy heart down there. It would have been especially nice if a Cornishman had taken on the tourists, for this year the county XV celebrates its centenary. It was formed in a Truro pub midway through the 1883–84 winter and played its first match against Devon on January 12, 1884. They were well beaten, though the *Western Daily Mercury* remarked that, 'One of the Cornish half-backs did much collaring.'

In those days Devon was one of the crack combinations in the country. Indeed, they were the first county ever to take on a team of touring All Blacks. The 1905 New Zealanders had arrived at Plymouth to report that they had saved their steamship from foundering off Cape Horn by helping to stoke the boilers 'for half a week when things looked bad' with an enduring shovelling rota of forwards and backs alike. After a wash-and-brush-up and two days rest to recover their land legs, they ran out for their first match.

Devon were expected to roll them over with ease. The result

buzzed up to London on the tapes. It was 4–55. The Fleet Street news agencies did not believe it and changed the information to Devon 55, New Zealand 4. That was released for the first editions. When confirmation came that the visitors had indeed been victorious, Fleet Street remained convinced that the score could only have been 4–5, and that was put out for second editions. We know better now.

Had they berthed at, say, Falmouth, and played Cornwall it might have been a different matter, for the boys of the Duchy had taken to the game with such a will that, three years later in 1908, and after only twenty-one years in the business, Cornwall were the *Olympic* rugger silver medallists! It is still on display at the St Ives RFC clubhouse.

It had been decided that England's county champions of the 1907–8 season would represent the country in the summer's Olympic Games at London's White City. Cornwall won the Championship in heroic style against Durham – then a stronghold of the game – and duly travelled by train to Paddington. They were met by all the county's Members of Parliament, who lunched them at the White City Garden Club – and then went out to be trounced by Australia by 32–3. Cornish rugger men have never travelled particularly well.

Through the Seventies I often had occasion to travel to Cornwall. If possible I would aim to go when the county were playing at home – preferably at Redruth. The granitey, hollocky old town would be abuzz for the afternoon's match. Miners and farmers and fishermen would do their shopping early. Boys would ride in on bikes from Penzance or Helston or Truro – bikes bedecked with the black and gold of old Cornwall like so many Wolverhampton Wanderers. Lunches in dingy pubs would sell like hot pasties. Then the crocodile queue would snake down to the ground, solemn men with hale faces and ancient, lived-in, coarse tweedy jackets and big boots laced with twine. They would all have a gleam of anticipation in their eye. The foreigners don't know what's going to 'it 'em, do uz. Any non-Cornishman is a blummun' foreigner.

The place to stand is 'Hellfire Corner', the corner-flag at the town end – the better to warm yourself in the throng, the better to witness in close-up the straining, heaving endeavours of the Cornish forwards, and the better, too, to keep your eye on the monument on the top of Carn Brea, the jagged hill that has stood sentinel over the town since time began. For they say that if you can see the monument it's going to rain – and if you can't see it, well, it must be raining already.

For rain is the bonus for Cornish rugger men. They are trained on it, and it runs in rivulets down to Hellfire Corner and there, preferably in the second-half (for Cornishmen prefer the dramatic unities), will the Cornish pack encamp, churning the mud and the spirits, till their will prevails. Being at Hellfire Corner when Cornwall get the winner in the final misty minutes is one of my most enduring, warming recollections in any sport. I've been in on it twice.

Down the years Cornwall have thrown up one or two players who have become household names. Talking of names, what about John MacGregor Kendall-Carpenter – five of them if you include the hyphen. He was a marvellous all-rounder. Another flanker for the litany was Vic Roberts, who captained England in the Fifties, and was given the Freedom of Penryn for, said the citation, 'bringing the name of the Town to the attention of the Nation'. And what about Richard Sharp, last in the line of the lovely, languid-striding, Corinthian fly-halves of olde Englande?

I never saw Cornwall's most legendary forward, the coalman, Bonzo Johns. Twenty-odd years ago, they say, he would finish his pony-and-cart delivery service round the town with just an hour to kick-off, grab a pasty on his way to the ground, tie up his nag at the railings and, without bothering to wipe the coaldust from his face or forearms, set about humping, heaving and horrifying every foreign front-row.

Bonzo came close, but was never picked for England. Stack Stevens was. He was another mighty prop. I knew Stack, not well but I knew him. He was another who trained on pasties and beer. He was a farmer up Godolphin way, between Helston and Marazion. A decade or so ago, when England teams began to be decorated in fancy tracksuits, Stack would have none of it. He'd turn up for England squad sessions in his jeans and when they pressed him into wearing the prissy garb, he'd decline – 'Sorry, sir, don't believe in tracksuits; s'pose I don't suffer from cold legs like as some I could mention.' They let him wear his jeans.

But Cornwall's most legendary player probably remains Bert Solomon. He was by all accounts a devastating centre-threequarter. He scored the try when the county won that Olympic silver medal in 1908. In Tom Salmon's centenary history of Cornish rugby – incidentally, just about the best of such labours of love that I have come across – he tells how Solomon played only once for England – against Wales in 1910, the year Twickenham was opened – and then declined all further selections because he felt so shy and uneasy in the company of the haughty public schoolboys who made up the rest of the international side.

On arrival at Twickenham his fly-half had asked him, 'I say, how do you like your passes, old man?' Bert had replied in his broad-as-Bodmin accent, 'Juss thraw the ball out, boy, an' I'll catch 'un.' Doubtless the rest of the England team had chortled at such an answer. At the post-match dinner Bert was asked where he went to school. Embarrassed, he turned his Trewirgie Boys' School (still going strong!) into Trewirgie *College*. He caught the milk train home and never again, I've heard it said, even replied to postcards pleading with him to play for England.

On the whole Cornishmen do not travel well east of the Tamar. Perhaps that's what the South-West selectors had in mind when they picked their team. Even Bristol would have been very foreign to Bert Solomon.

Black Watch

The West Indian cricketers are touring again. Old ones and loved ones – and feared ones – are back. Men like Joel Garner, the Big Bird with the melon smile who is different in that he genuinely dislikes softening up batsmen with bumpers (though that doesn't always stop him), and the *nonpareil* with the patrician's profile, Vivian Isaac Alexander Richards. What Christian names for an emperor!

But as at the start of any tour, half the party are bursting to make their names. Somebody always does. They say a boy, Richardson, is the bat to watch. A few old faces have gone from the XI that in recent years made up probably the most relentlessly powerful side in the game's international history – based on an unceasing, cruel barrage of fast bowling. They were just about invincible, though purists would call their sides of the Fifties and Sixties far better, balanced as they were by such wizards of tweak and cunning as Ramadhin and Valentine, Gibbs and, of course, the one and only Sobers, of the power and the glory, the charm and the infinite variety.

With Lloyd, the long, languid, glinting, hunched old beanpole, in such consummate charge, it is hard to believe that only a quarter of a century ago there was a right old racial to-do round the islands when Frank Worrell became the first black man to captain their cricket team. And it was not much more than half a century ago that even Neville Cardus was patronizing about them being allowed an official tour of England in 1928. 'The fellows,' he wrote, 'will not be up to it.' Then he saw Learie Constantine bat and bowl and field.

When I was last in Trinidad I caught the bus from Port-of-Spain to Maraval, a teeny village encased in sheer-drop, dreamy, steamy, forested hills. The pilgrimage took me up the raggedy Morne Coco Lane. Half-way up, on an overgrown, tumbledown patch, four simple concrete steps, almost lost amid the weeds and grasses, showed that a house was once there. It was once the shack where, in 1903, a black boy had been born. All his grandparents had been slaves.

The boy had learned his cricket here. In time he was to become the first Negro Peer in history to sit in the House of Lords. Baron of Maraval. I sat on those stone steps and read the Cardus cutting I had brought from England: 'Learie Constantine's cricket was a prophecy that has gloriously come to pass: for it forecast, by its mingled skill, daring, absolutely un-English trust to instinct, and by its dazzling flashes of physical energy, the coming one day of Weekes, of Worrell, of Headley, of Walcott, of Kanhai, of Sobers. All of these cricketers remain, for all their acquired culture and ordered technique, descendants of Learie, cricketers in Learie's lineage.'

Already add to that list – Lloyd, Richards, Garner . . .

That first trip of mine to the Caribbean was a heady one. I attended, with the rest of the current West Indies team, a moving memorial birthday service at Sir Frank Worrell's serene and lonely grave high above the sea at Bridgetown. I sat next to Clyde Walcott at supper; he is grey-haired now, a sombre pinstriped official, but still a great bear of a man. Everton Weekes actually bought me a drink: he is now the champion Barbados *bridge* player. In Jamaica I saw Graham Gooch score a century for England in the company of a white-haired, squat old man with soft-boiled, bloodshot eyes. He kept doling out boiled sweets and oohed and aahed with glee at every trenchant stroke. He was George Headley, perhaps the best of them all, Richards notwithstanding.

I went to visit Sonny Ramadhin's aunt, down in Naipaul country, in the south of Trinidad near San Fernando – where they really have erected on a plinth in the town centre the very last train engine that ran from Port-of-Spain before they ripped up the rails . . . Ramadhin was the mystic spin bowler who later became the much loved owner of a pub in Saddleworth, Lancashire. His Aunt Sumintra's little wooden house on stilts has become a sort of shrine to her nephew. The walls are covered in sepia snapshots, each lovingly framed in passepartout.

Before the boy left to mesmerize the English, and the world, in 1950, he had played in only two first-class games of cricket. On the wall is a studio study of him the day he left; he was wearing a trilby-type titfer on the back of his head and he looks as solemnly sinister as a Hollywood extra playing a Chinatown hood. There is also a picture of a starchy white-tie-and-tails banquet at London's Café Royal during that first tour. Sonny is the only diner of hundreds wearing an ordinary necktie.

I had seen them all for the first time that summer thirty-four years ago. It seemed the whole village caught the dawn bus from outside Woolworth's in Stroud to ring the railings of the Cheltenham College Ground. They were the first black men that most of us had ever seen. Weekes made a dazzling half century, and Walcott a frightening, thrilling century off his back foot. Then those two little pals, Ramadhin and Valentine, bowled Gloucester heroes out for next to nothing.

Since when, of course, I have read the history books that deal with even earlier stuff. And found how appropriate and fair it was that Gloucester were so well beaten on that famous day.

In 1900, an English colonial, Aucher Warner, brother of Sir Pelham, had brought over a West Indian touring team to England. It included just a handful of black makeweight players, including two fast bowlers, Woods and Cumberbatch. On June 28 they played a one-day game against Gloucestershire at Bristol. The county's legendary, scientific hitter, Jessop, flayed them for 157 within the hour. At the height of the onslaught, Woods approached Warner to ask if he could remove his boots. He never played with them at home. 'I can get him, sir, if you only let me feel de pitch with me toes.'

Warner was horrified. 'Certainly not, sir! This is England! And another thing, you are playing a first-class county, sir!'

Woods continued in his boots. And Jessop continued his cruel lesson.

I always fancy that somewhere the likes of Constantine and Martindale, Hall and Griffith, Holding, Roberts and Garner, have heard that story – and have ever since been bowling at Englishmen with dear old Woods and Cumberbatch in mind.

Hold on to your helmets!

Lions Among Lambs

New Zealand as British as the British? Don't jest: It's far more British than the British. Even the climate would have Michael 'Scattered Showers' Fish donning his gaudiest, most joyful necktie: it's sunnier than Britain, also wetter and windier – and, for good measure, far more woolly with sheep. Regularly each day, in everything from cuisine to culture, you are warped back in time a full quarter of a century and more. Meat and fish always come with two veg and gravy. Coffee is Camp, tea is high, Church is low, and brows are middling.

Both channels of the national television service are smug, bland and patronizing, like Auntie in the 1950s. Today in New Zealand 'Coronation Street' runs a few years late. The wireless hawks an unending drone of Matt Monro, Lita Roza, and Cliff in puberty, interrupted occasionally by 'rush-hour' traffic dramas that, honestly, report such as: 'There are two sheep loose on the grass verges at Ruwahini Road.' In the small, grid-square, market towns that they call cities – like Wanganui, Rotorua or Hamilton North – every third shop is titled such as 'The Yarn Barn' or 'Knitwits' and given over to selling knitting needles and patterns. There is also an obvious craze and demand for waterbeds, bought from emporiums called 'Dream Machine' or 'Cosy'n'Co.' Something racier like 'Wet Dream' wouldn't go down well in Godzone, which is every native's nickname for their dear and beloved land. The smallest town has a war memorial listing a long, and almost incredible, litany of men killed in two wars, defending a tiny group of islands off Europe and a million miles away.

Beatrice Webb called Kiwis 'the most provincial people on the face of the earth', and that can be seen now as the only enduring truism she ever bleated from Bloomsbury. New Zealanders are outdoor folk, hale and healthy and purple-cheeked from the sun and the winds. Indoors, they call any party quorum of more than five 'a function' – except once, when I was sent a handsomely printed invitation to a 'cheese 'n' biccy spread'. At a 'function' you must wear a club tie that you are prepared to swop, and ideally be dressed in a tent-slack blazer attached to a massive, wire-gilt club badge of horrendous heraldic design. No subjects anywhere stand more straight-backed for 'God Save the Queen'.

New Zealanders are extremely kind, warm and over-generous. Nothing is too much trouble. In hardware stores, door-mats sell best with 'welcome' on them. Like Olde England used to be, it's a man's world. *Guardian* Woman hunts not here. Naked Apes roam free. Women past thirty pour tea, grow rhododendrons, and visit the knitting-needle shop on the way to their weekly perm booking at a barber's called 'Vanity Fair' or 'Sophisticut'. The young girls have open, laughing faces and their ready smiles are unredded by Max Factor's smarmy smears. They are uncomplicated, enchantingly guileless and endearingly careless and carefree about coupling or the Curse. They are far better-read than their men. They just want to be mums. They are mountainously broad in the beam, but no publisher would dream of starting a slimmer's weekly here.

Yet, in a hundred-odd years of history, these happy, homely women are responsible for breeding successive line upon line of rampaging, bloodthirsty, young warrior tribesmen. Settlers' wars had nothing on the ritual – about twice a decade – that has this hand-picked elite brigade of natives, woading themselves in liniment and Vaseline, buckling on symbolic armour of All-Black and going for the visiting British in a brutal assault of savage intensity which is as frightening as it is colonially heroic. The trampling, highly trained All Blacks against the once haughty, crimson-shirted British Lions is not a pretty sight, and for a century the beleaguered, thin, red line has scarcely ever held.

This South Seas' winter sees the unfair battles waged again. Only once – in 1971 – has a series been won by the combined British Rugby Union team of the best that England, Wales, Scotland and All-Ireland can muster. They play, for obvious reasons, in red shirts, white shorts, and stockings of blue and green. The first tour of Brits was in 1888, by English and Scottish public schoolboys, with the cricketers, Shaw, Shrewsbury and Lillywhite, raising the loot and the travelling 'sponsorships' from private businesses in London. They were beaten by club sides, but there was no official international match, for the New Zealand Rugby Union was not formed till four years later.

The game had been introduced by Charles John Monro, a tearaway young laddo whose early rumbustiousness is belied by the bewhiskered, Edwardian solemnity with which he stares out of his gilded portrait frames that are hung on most New Zealand rugby clubhouse walls. He was the son of Sir David Monro, the speaker in the country's first House of Representatives. Young Charles was getting a skimpy education in the South Island settlement of Nelson in 1867 when, at fifteen, his father sent him for a dose of muscular Christianity in England; he spent three years at Christ's College, Finchley, in North London, and played a code of football that originated from the Rugby School of William

Webb Ellis. He was more enthusiastic, wide-eyed, and rustic than his contemporaries, but played for the school's reserve team. Three years later he returned to Nelson and persuaded his mates at the local 'Association' club to give a go to his discovery of a 'hacking and handling' game. Within a year they had crossed Cook Strait to the capital city where they played a match against fifteen young men of Wellington. Suddenly, these faraway farmers had found other flocks to kill.

The Maoris, too, took to the game with equal ferocity. In 1904 a British side won handsomely all their thirteen games in Australia, then travelled across the Tasman Sea to be surprisingly well beaten twice in New Zealand. In the following year a full, official, mixed-race, New Zealand team visited Britain. They were given no chance at all. On the way over, their steamship almost foundered off Cape Horn, being saved only by the team helping to stoke the boilers for two successive days with a desperate, unending gusto. They docked at Plymouth and at once played Devon, who were expected to roll them over with ease. The result was 55–4. The Fleet Street news agencies did not believe it and changed the information to Devon 55, New Zealand 4. When confirmation came that the visitors had indeed been victorious, Fleet Stret still was certain the score could only have been 5–4, which was the result they released for second editions.

Then continued a trail of runaway victories around the land. They played in black shirts, but their nickname remained 'The Kiwis'. In their sixth game at Hartlepool – then a stronghold of the Union game – they won by 63–0, and a leading London writer of the day, a Mr Vivian, tried to explain before the match that the secret of the upstarts' game was based on each man being very fit, fast and athletic, unlike the British tradition of lumbering, butter-fingered forwards, and darting, dainty backs. Pronounced Vivian: 'They are all backs.' When the billboard announcing this legend was sent up with the newspaper train to Hartlepool, the local newsagent could not understand it. But he knew the colour of the tourists' shirts. He changed all the billings to 'They are all blacks.' The name stuck – as did another for that same mesmerizing colonial team of 1905: 'The Invincibles'.

Thereafter, the only time the New Zealanders played in

white was at home in 1930, the first time the British Lions were so named on Twickenham's headed notepaper. Again a journalist had inspired it – when a British side had attempted to maul the 'Springboks' of South Africa two years before.

In 1930, ninety-seven British players were approached before a final party of twenty-nine could be assembled. Not many could take off two-thirds of a year for however stimulating an adventure. It was only on the eve of the team's departure from Southampton that the Leicester international, F. D. Prentice, was told to captain the side – and he was presented with a laundry hamper containing thirty royal-blue shirts, each crested by three gilt lions rampant. So when the game began the All Blacks changed to white. By 1950 the mother country wore red.

It made no difference – the Brits were trampled underfoot again. Now, more than fifty years on, the boys in black will come down from their green-grey, sheep-speckled hills to stifle another invasion from the Redcoats.

Their gentle, homely, hair-permed womenfolk will encourage them in silent content, needles clacking away – though for the few weeks it's as if they're knitting alongside the guillotine. And all appropriately to the strains of Mr Matt Monro.

SOCCER SYNDROME

A Fair Kop

The 1984 Milk (née League) Cup Final marked the first time Liverpool and Everton met at Wembley. It was to be Everton's opportunity to scotch at last the painful, long-time jibes from half Merseyside about their inability to win even an egg cup. For years the seedy old concrete pile has been Liverpool's second home.

As Bill Shankly once growled at someone who described Everton as the city's second best team: 'Nonsense! Second best is easily Liverpool Reserves!'

It is astonishing that English soccer's old firm have never before met in a Cup Final. Mind you, Liverpool would not even have existed but for Everton. A century ago St Domingo's Sunday School team bagged a pitch in Stanley Park when it was first opened to the public. They called themselves 'Everton' and were sponsored by the Conservative MP and brewer, John Houlding. He charged them a nominal one hundred pounds per annum for rent. The ground was called 'Anfield'. When, four years later in 1888, they joined the newly-formed Football League and were able to charge admission money, Houlding upped the rent to £250 and demanded exclusive rights to sell refreshments. Capital capitalism.

St Domingo's committee offered the MP £180. Livid, he threw them out on the spot. They moved to some scrubland on the north side of Stanley Park, described as having 'degenerated from a nursery to a howling desert' – but in no time they had transformed it into 'Goodison Stadium' and in 1892 Lord Kinnaird, FA bigwig, opened it with a firework display. By the end of the century it was the best equipped ground in the land. And Everton one of the best teams.

Meanwhile, still furious, Houlding had recruited a new team for himself at Anfield. He still insisted on calling it 'Everton', but both the Football League and the FA demanded he change it. Grandly, he baptized his side 'Liverpool', and when the existing rugby union club of that name complained, Houlding simply stuck *AFC* on the end.

The first local derby was played in 1894 – Everton won 3–0 at Goodison. In that game, Liverpool's colours were 'royal blue and white quarters', and Everton played in 'ruby vests'. I can trace no reason why, only two years later, both clubs' colours were exactly the reverse. They have been the Reds and the Blues ever since.

Liverpool's more homely Anfield has never matched the grandeur of Goodison. But Anfield's 'Kop' is not only the most famous but the very first. Now, if even the most humble Isthmian League side has the tiniest hillock of clinkered standing room behind a goal, they call it 'the Kop'. In 1906 Liverpool extended Anfield and built up their terracing on the south side.

Six years earlier, in the Boer War, 322 British soldiers had been massacred while trying to capture a hill in South Africa called Spion Kop. The attempt had been a complete shambles. Leading the charge were members of the 2nd Lancashire Regiment and Fusiliers. When Anfield built their terracing, a sporting journalist on the local *Post & Echo*, Ernest Edwards, suggested calling it 'Spion Kop' as a memorial to the soldier supporters who had been killed.

Two world wars went by before Liverpool consistently challenged Everton as Merseyside's leading team. Liverpool had their moments, but Everton had a glorious string of success through the 1920s and '30s when Dixie Dean first led their line and then nursed Tom Lawton to take up the flag. Dean remains history's most dashing and regular goal-scoring centre-forward: rumbustious, courageous, wide-shouldered, delicate-footed, with the classic No. 9's Brylcreemed centre-parting that could head the ball with astonishing power.

It was said that, say before a derby match, he would be strolling down to the pub for a snack and a midday game of darts and he would nod across the street to the Liverpool goalie, Elisha Scott – which would cause Elisha, on reflex, to dive straight through a plate-glass shopfront.

After 1945, Liverpool still took some years to get their bearings. They were itsy-bitsy, up and down, even when they sported the charms of that consummate Scottish winger, Billy Liddell. For a long time they were called *Liddelpool*, rather in the manner that Glos CCC used to be known as *Proctershire*. For a few seasons a Liverpool favourite of those days was a tearaway ginger nut of a centre-forward by the name of Albert Stubbins. His job, any old how, to get on the end of Liddell's crosses. Liverpool had just been relegated to the Second Division and not doing too well. In those days the two lowest divisions were broken up geographically into Third, north and south.

Over came this Liddell centre. Stubbins soared, but mis-timed the leather and his forehead hit the crossbar with an almighty clang. He was stretchered off and an ambulance took him to the city's Royal Northern Hospital.

Some hours later he woke up. A nurse was by his bedside. 'Where am I?' mumbled Albert.

'Don't worry, duck,' said the nurse, 'you're in the Northern.'

Albert opened an eye. 'We didn't,' he said, 'stay long in the Second, did we?'

Nose to the Ground

They stand there, wide, green, empty caverns, used barely once or twice a fortnight. They are modern cathedrals, each cornered by four Meccano spires that spear to the sky. There are ninety-two of them. They are the football grounds of England.

In most cases they are attended on a Saturday afternooon by more people than, the following morning, go to all the local churches put together. And yet drear and dusty architectural manuals through the years recite and regurgitate dull details about the most insignificant church. Nikolaus Pevsner, in his acclaimed and apparently classicly comprehensive guide to *The Buildings of England*, mentions only in minute passing two football grounds, those at Wembley in North London and Hillsborough in Sheffield. He describes the perambulation of the suburb of Everton, in Liverpool, mentioning churches, parks and public buildings, but walks past the solid mass of Goodison Park as if it didn't exist. Similarly in London's Highbury, there is no fractional indication that he even recognizes the presence of Arsenal FC – though, on second thoughts, these days that might be understandable.

Soccer's most eminent historian probably remains Percy Young. A couple of decades ago he wrote, 'There are some who "collect" theatres . . . or it may be railway stations . . . some day some scholar will arrive at the conclusion that there remains one definitive work still to be written: on the architecture of football grounds.' And so it has come to pass.

Quite simply, Simon Inglis' *Football Grounds of England and Wales* is a triumph.

Inglis, a Manchester freelance journalist, has the perfect credentials: he is a devoted nut about both soccer and architecture. He is a swot with songs to sing and marvellous titbit tales to tell. That rare bird who is told to 'Shush!' giggling in the reference library. He is also hot stuff on weights, measures, geometry and cantilevers.

He sets out his stall at once: 'Anyone who has been to a football match will know that rush of excitement when first catching sight of the floodlights and stands. Once inside there is an almost exultant feeling as you emerge onto the terrace or into the stand, and see the arena for the first time. The experience of visiting a football ground is inseparable from the game itself, for every ground provides a different backdrop and a different atmosphere colouring your entire appreciation of the match. . . . The lover of football grounds will pass through a town, by train or car, and strain to see floodlights on the horizon. The merest glimpse of a stand or a pitch is tantalizing.' And so it is.

He takes no sides, nor tips his hat to bigwigs. He approaches Aldershot with all the awe in which he walks to Anfield. I wish he could have substantiated the tale of the Third Division manager who, as the main stand burned to the ground, delayed the arrival of fire engines in the hope that the insurance might buy him a new team; or of how an aggrieved groundsman who had been dismissed refused to tell the new incumbent where the underground taps were situated, resulting in the need to dig up the pitch in a treasure hunt.

Inglis himself mines deep for the quaint and the quirky. There is a throwaway gem or two on every one of his 272 pages. Talking of arson, one is inclined to believe the above story happened at least once, for there seems to have been a heck of a lot of grandstand fires over the century. Notes Inglis: 'The one which destroyed the Main Stand at St James' Park, Exeter, on November 17, 1925, also ignited all the players' kit, except for Bob Pollard's boots, which were being repaired in Northampton.' There's research for you.

In the dear, dead days of the Fifties I had occasion quite often to visit Bristol City on carefree, frostbitten afternoons when the chirpy, red, red Robins were bob-bob-bobbing along with the likes of Bradford and Atyeo. We used to stand at the Covered End in front of the Winterstoke Road entrance. Inglis pulled me up with a blushing jolt. 'In the club's early years there were two stands on either side of the pitch, No. 1 and No. 2 Stands, but the first development as we know it today was at the Winterstoke Road End, built in the late 1920s after the sale of two players, Keating and Bourton, for £3,000. For a while it was called *The Keating Stand*.' My italics!

Of the twelve original member clubs of the Football League, which was formed in 1888, only three still use the same grounds they occupied then – Stoke City ('in the 1970s they began to compete in Europe, and almost as a reminder not to get too carried away by success, a gale carried away the roof of the Butler St Stand'); Preston North End ('in 1936 the firm of Abbotts in Lancaster installed specially designed stained-glass windows in the boardroom, and not even Highbury had those'); and Burnley ('Turf Moor is believed to be the first football ground ever visited by a member of the Royal Family when, in October 1886, having just opened the nearby Victoria Hospital, the Queen's son, Prince Albert, watched Burnley v Bolton in the company of 9,000 others, some paying a guinea to sit nearest the Royal party').

In spite of the definition of his title, Inglis is such an enthusiast he cannot resist a peek into Scotland. A paragraph on the opening of Celtic's Parkhead ground in 1892 – 'As the Irish patriot, Michael Davitt, laid the first turf he recited, "On alien soil like yourself I am here/I'll take root and flourish, of that never fear" ' – reminds me of the young Celtic goalkeeper, John Thomson, who died in 1931 after diving at the feet of a Rangers' forward. Thomson was the only member of that Celtic side who was a Protestant.

In an earlier match against Rangers, he was leaving the field at half-time with a colleague, McGrory, and the conversation went, as they say, something like this:

Thomson: That centre-forward of theirs keeps calling me a seethin' Papist bastard.

McGrory: Don't let that bother you, I get called that and worse every week.

Thomson: That's all right for you, you are one!

Close Network

Frank Swift was the first goalkeeper to dominate the six-yard box of my consciousness. He had hands as big as Joe Baksi and, on tiptoe, the peak of his cap could touch the crossbar. Raymond Glendenning would always describe him on the wireless as 'the big fellow'. Then came the first colour photographs, and a shot of Bert Williams turning one round for a corner, wings outstretched in flight like a tacking Spitfire, inspired me to ask my mother to knit me a similar polo-neck jumper of canary yellow.

Swift became a journalist and, representing the *News of the World*, died in the Munich air crash in 1958. The last I heard of Williams he was headmaster of a School for Goalkeepers in the Black Country. In the earlyish 1950s Bert vied for the yellow badge of courage with another Midlander, Gil Merrick, who in the space of three hours on either side of Christmas 1953, let in thirteen goals against Hungary. Thereafter, with his sad toothbrush moustache and spaniel eyes, he always looked like the boxer, Jack Gardner, when Bruce Woodcock was hitting him.

Back in the mists they were called 'net-minders'. In an essay on his craft in 1900, the Southampton polo-neck, Jack Robinson, began: 'We do not grow on trees. Many imagine us custodians of the sticks are as plentiful as berries in autumn. I concede there are thousands who consider themselves keepers of the goal, but you must remember there are thousands upon thousands of men who consider themselves poets. And just as there are poets and poets so there are goalkeepers and goalkeepers.' Quite.

Far earlier than that, in *Football at Westminster School*, H. C. Benham had defined the very beginnings for every mittened Horatius. 'A goalkeeper is a duffer or funk-stick. If any player who was playing out showed any sign of funk or failed to play up, he was packed off into goal at once, not only for that day, but as a lasting degradation. On the other hand, if any keeper made a good save of a goal, he was called for immediately to play out, and thenceforth he played out always.'

Since when, of course, the Netminders' Union has become a pretty closed shop. It is not in the least bit chauvinist to say the British have been remarkably well blessed. Offhand, since Glendenning's 'big fellow', I can rattle off a litany of last-liners – Hopkinson and Hodgkinson, Swindin and Bartram, Springett and Ditchburn, Kelsey and Sprake, Uprichard and Gregg, Lawrence and Stepney and Brown. Not forgetting Bonetti 'The Cat' . . . nor Montgomery of the Sunderland save . . .

Oddly, Scotland have seldom fielded reliable hundred per centers. Their glorious talents are reserved for those playing 'out'. I suppose the most celebrated tartan goalie remains John Thomson, who was capped at twenty-two in 1930 but a year later died after diving at the feet of a Ranger. At his memorial

service, the theme of the requiem was, 'Greater love hath no man than that he lay down his life for his friends.' His ghost is said still to haunt the six-yard box at Celtic. On braw and wintry full-moon nights at Celtic Park you can still, apparently, hear the eerie, desperate, high-pitched shriek of 'Mine!'

My own particular favourite was the Fulham gloveman a quarter of a century past. When Tony Macedo was good he was very, very good – but when . . . But we loved him. He once lost us a semi-final of the Cup. But we knew he'd got us there in the first place. He was a magnificent madcap. The old *Manchester Guardian* football correspondent, H. D. Davies, may well have seen Macedo the week before he wrote that it was 'axiomatic that goalkeepers, like wicketkeepers, were "a slate loose".'

Then Gordon Banks rewrote the rules, re-drew the geometry, upped even the courage. I was in Mexico for the 1970 World Cup, but was covering another match and never saw for real Banks' save against Pele, of Brazil and the Universe. On television it is all over and done with in a blurr. But the journalist, John Moynihan, was actually behind Banks' net as:

'Pele hurtled in, leaping over Mullery, and all for one were shouting "Goal!" and rising to acclaim the "King". Then an outrageous flash of movement, a combination of sprawling arms and legs. Banks was suddenly over to the right of goal lying sideways with his left leg thrust out straight, his other bent at right angles and his groping right hand scooping the ball up and over the crossbar. Banks, in this attitude of a praying mantis after spinning to a new twig, had played the ball up and away with an extended palm into oblivion. It tumbled over the bar and rolled slowly onto the other side of the net with the sudden abatement of an ocean wave after breaking on a rock. And one wondered, amid all the shouting and screaming and commotion, whether England's goalkeeper had broken his arm and suffered grievous damage; he lay on his back with his shoulders on the grass, his colleagues standing around too nonplussed to yell their praise. Already the moment had become a legend, a piece of unique folklore, a gymnastic impossibility. "Did you see that!" roared Harry, turning round to me. His nicotined fingers were trembling with tension. "Christ! Did you see that'!"

Clemence and Corrigan were taking turns in Banks' jumper

by the time the hero lost an eye in a motor accident. Now England's Peter Shilton, geometry and agility allied to a rousing, bullying, muscular presence, is considered one of the best in the world and a formidable successor to Banks.

And yet, there remains a goalkeeper who plays, week in, week out, in the English Football League, who might, when grandchildren come to write history books, figure with far more twirly gold-leaf script. Up among the jerseyed gods will be Pat Jennings, once of Watford and Tottenham Hotspur, now of Arsenal. He recently played his hundredth game in goal for Northern Ireland.

Jennings, still the same soft and gentle fellow who came over from Newry twenty years ago, is thirty-eight now. He cannot have long times left between the sticks. If fathers care about such things they should summon their sons and go to see Jennings keep goal before he picks up the gloves from the back of his net for the last time, shakes hands with his opposite number in the wintry sunset, and clatters down the tunnel forever.

Like Swift and Williams of my boyhood, Jennings keeps guard of his cluttered stage of bodies and boots and braying, brawling, breathlessness, with athleticism, bravery, grace and chivalry. The olde tyme hero. And I always fancy he, too, plays even that teeny bit better in his yellow jersey.

Fast Forwards

There is just a month between them: Trevor Brooking was born in October, 1948, and Mike Channon in November. There is just one England cap between them: Brooking has forty-seven, Channon forty-six. In the admittedly dreary dozen or so years since England had a national soccer side that seemed to know exactly where the goalposts were, the two of them, more often than not, could display a singular turn of talent. They were often seen to be smiling; and when they were fouled they didn't foul back.

From the top of the stand of a murky, phosphorescent teatime, you would half-close your eyes to a squint and still tell them from the others by their gait – something you cannot do with too many mundane midfield men these days. Both were gallopers: Channon was the thoroughbred, classic, short sprinter; Brooking, who had a caressing touch on the ball, lolloped more like a stayer. Neither, alas, had quite the flamboyant nature nor the cruel competitive edge to take a game by the throat and throttle it to submission. But often and gaily they decorated many people's Saturday afternoons.

In 'Close Network' I suggested that, if fathers care about such things, they should summon their sons and go to see Pat Jennings – at thirty-eight, three years older than these two forwards – keep goal for Arsenal just once more before he picks up the gloves from the back of his net for the last time and clatters down the tunnel for ever. The same applies here. Hurry, hurry, while such stocks last.

The 1983–84 season was Brooking's last. And no Dame Nellie Bugner he. Channon says he feels like frolicking for a few years yet, but old athletes' bones are brittle and there's no knowing how long they can keep up the chase. And if his zip goes, then surely will his zap.

Brooking joined West Ham as an apprentice in 1965, a year before Hurst, Moore, and Peters helped win the World Cup for England. He arrived with eleven O-levels and A-levels in Economics and Accountancy. Before the Sixties were over he had set up his own firm in the plastics trade. It has flourished. He has no remote desire to try his hand at soccer club management. He has his feet on the ground. A shrewd East Ender. His mother and father met when they both worked for the Co-op at Barking. Dad later became a police sergeant. On those faraway Fifties Saturdays every available policeman for miles around was not drafted with their handcuffs to Upton Park. After the boy's tenth birthday Sergeant Brooking would take him, hand in hand, to stand at the North Bank terraces for every home match. 'There was a friendly, family atmosphere,

and a tingling, wholesome excitement. If I had a son of ten today I wouldn't take him near it. It's so sad.'

Later, on that same field, the lumbering jogtrot was actually deceptive. It allowed Brooking a placid, not to say serene, journey to the right place at the right time. For all his schemes were born of a sharp, clear awareness. When he was fouled he looked pained, not for himself but for the juvenile boorishness of his marker. He once scored the winning goal in a Cup final with a genuflecting header – such an unlikely event that it kept all Essex warm with delight throughout the bad summer that followed. And he could occasionally hit some screamers with either instep, especially with his right. Once, in Budapest for England, a twenty-odd yarder clamped itself to the net stanchion and the poor Hungarian goal-keeper took a minute or two to prise the thing away.

Channon, too, has logged some dramatic whizzbangs in his time, not least for Norwich City. He also played for Manchester City in a side that could, and should, have been an enlightening one. But it is always as a Southampton Saint that he will be remembered. Nothing really, but when he first played for England in 1972 I recall being charmed by the fact that he had a broad Wessex accent. Somehow, you don't associate the growly burr and the buzz with top flight soccer. To go with it was a hale and handsome, boyish, countryman's face; and a trim, lithe figure, and a speed that blistered off the mark; and then sometimes, in the sternest hullabaloo, the broad, toothy smile.

He was born at Orcheston, a farming village on the Plain. Around full moons, on a clear night, you could see Stonehenge. It was equidistant, thirty miles each way, between Swindon and Southampton. The boy was still in single figures when Dad took him to the local derby at Southampton's Dell. He couldn't see a thing, and doesn't think he enjoyed it much. But his father did, and in future when they went, they stood at the back of the terracing so son could sit on father's shoulders.

At Amesbury School, he played for Wiltshire Boys. After a match against Hampshire on the little Walled Meadow in Andover, two of the few grand old legends of Wessex football, Bert Head, the manager of Swindon, and Ted Bates, his counterpart at Southampton, met, with smiles, to haggle. Ted won, and the scrawny fifteen-year-old sprinter found himself in digs in Southampton within days.

Channon is still the countryman, the wide-eyed Jude enjoying the bigtime only while it lasts. His hobby has turned into a small business: he owns and breeds racehorses.

Trevor Brooking, in his pinstripes and patent leather briefcase, might well exchange every one of his England caps to be named Young Plastics Businessman of the Year. Mike Channon would certainly swop every one of his, to own a Derby winner. So far, in the Classics anyway, they cannot run as fast as he could.

Suffolk Punch

In the last dozen years – in which Ipswich only twice finished out of the First Division's top ten, and won the FA Cup, gloriously, and the UEFA Cup – Portman Road's cheery buzz was the sound to be in on. I've had no end of splendid Saturdays there: a lie-in, then leisurely to the 11.30 buffet special from London's Liverpool Street; a stroll to the city centre, a browse in that bookshop, then perhaps a gammon 'n' pineapple platter at Berni's or a chop 'n' fried egg at the snackerie of the Great White Horse, where Dickens once stayed.

The air was Eastern sharp, but even the visiting yobs seemed mellow. The match seemed always tingling tense and fresh. The Ipswich team played with a mixture of perspiring gusto, hale straightforwardness and only occasional guile. They would charge in waves: Lambert and Whymark and Johnson, then Morris, Talbot and Mills would be followed by Hunter and Beattie's burly mob. My favourite was the cleverest – a spindly, arrogant, inconsistent, sparky blond winger called Woods. Later came the likes of Brazil, Mariner and Wark, and the two Dutchmen, Muhren and Thijssen. All gone West now.

But it was after the match, in the boardroom, that you really twigged the Ipswich philosophy. It was open house to every hick and hack. With all other League clubs, you must realize, such inner sanctums seem exclusive to the smarm of smoothy salesmen and the humbug of civic dignity. At

Ipswich the post-match junket was presided over by the brewing family Cobbold, to whom the fun of Saturday afternoon footer was just a diversion from the fun of the rest of the week.

To all intents, the club was pioneered by Captain Ivan Cobbold, who laid in with his love and his loot when the side was amiably booting around the basement of the amateur Southern League in the middle 1930s. By 1938 they were elected to the Football League when Capt. Ivan bought them a secondhand tin grandstand from the Newmarket Racecourse. The ground was badly bombed during the war – but not as conclusively as poor Captain Ivan, who was killed in the air raid on the Guards' Chapel, London, in 1944.

He left two sons. When soccer resumed, first an uncle then a cousin kept warm the big seat for the eldest, John, who at twenty-six became the League's youngest chairman in 1953. Nothing at ITFC was ever the same, whichever way you like to look at it. From day one the Old Etonian was pouring the drinks for the hicks and the hacks.

He appointed as manager Alf Ramsey, hot from the Hotspurs, and at once the *charmant*, happy-go-lucky brewer touched an inspired chord in the sombre, shy, determined former full-back. In five seasons Ipswich not only careered out of the Third Division, South, but won promotion to the First and, lo and behold, came top of that.

When Ramsey left to turn similar tricks for the English national team, Mr John threw a swank and swilling celebration banquet. During his thank-you speech, the yet unknighted Alf was droning on and on in his monotonous, elocuted, over-rehearsed strain when a mystery voice was heard to be repeatedly heckling below him, *under* the top table: 'C'mon Ramsey, stop it there . . . stop boring everyone . . . enough's enough, Alfie baby . . .' It was his very special chairman taking a carpet breather.

Bobby Robson came. His carefree chairman nursed him through rough rides, till the successes became more regular. That is when I started travelling with them to competitions in Europe. The team were led invariably through the Customs gates by Mr John, in his tweedy old suit with half mast trousers, his rumpled Guards' tie, his filthy Hush Puppies – and all to the clink of his Duty Frees in the bright yellow plastic bag. Once, in East Germany I think, the team had made a spectacular second-leg recovery, and I somehow was first to finish telephoning the deathless clichés back to London. In the Press room I came across Mr John being interviewed by the local, earnest, Germanic TV and Press. He was clutching the statutory visiting chairman's presentation gift of Cellophaned flowers.

How do you feel, sir, after the great victory? was the pidgin-English tone of the guttural question. Mr John looked at the journalist, then down at the flowers. 'Tell you the truth, Fritz, I feel an absolute wanker holding these, an *absolute* pisspot!' The German solemnly wrote it all down in shorthand.

Once, when Ipswich beat the Italian club, Lazio, in Rome after being almost kicked to pieces on the pitch, we arrived back at Heathrow next morning to hear that the Football Association had made the strongest representations about the Italians' thuggery etc., etc. All the usual guff. Anyway, it was a big story and ITN jostled with BBC for the chairman's airport comments. Will you, they asked, be pulling out of European competition as a protest unless Lazio are banned? 'Of course not, old boy,' replied Mr John, 'how else do you expect us to stock up on our Duty Frees!'

Mr John died last year. He was mourned at many stations past Ipswich. His younger brother, Patrick, had long since taken over as chairman, but the same philosophy and fun held good. As Mr John once told me: 'There was no truth in the rumour that Bobby Robson ran the Ipswich team single-handed. On the contrary, I was the ruthless dictator – I telephoned him every morning to say "What's on your mind, Bob?" He told me everything, and then I barked out my orders. They were the same every day. They were "Right, carry on then".'

One teatime, after a game against the Spurs I think, Mr John brought a young punk into the oak-panelled boardroom. He could have been no more than sixteen or seventeen. The chairman showed him every item in the trophy cabinet then poured him a large slug of whisky. 'Now you go back to London,' he told the kid, 'and tell them how nice we are up here at Ipswich Town.'

Replied the spike-haired boy: 'London? I comes from Wickham Market, meself.'

Final Chorus

At the 1984 FA Cup Final between Watford and Everton they could have done worse than invite Elton John down from the Royal Box to sort out the sing-song before the start of the match. Watford had never been to Wembley before. Their chairman might just have had the rhythm, or at least sense of occasion, to improve the pre-match choral standards on the terraces. At any rate, one suspects, the moon-faced little ivory tinkler with the great big nil-nil specs and the boater that hides the Boycott hair-knit, would not have panicked and walked off early from the rostrum in an embarrassed huff like some of the FA's hired cheerleaders over the years.

No section sings the same song, and anyway most of the words come out smelling of raspberries. To think they used to hand out hymn sheets with the programme. 'God Save Our Gracious Team' is the mildest of the lyrics.

'Community Singing will commence at 2 o'clock,' is how the scoutmasterly Football Association persevere in billing their programme. *Us* to *Them* on how to behave on the day of days. It remains the perfect example for the Two-Nation theorists: to witness the grandstand patricians in their Sunday suits rising from their Saturday seats to sing the Anthem or 'Abide with Me' as shoals of proles on the teraces look to drown the pomp with workers' whistles and ripe obscenities. The Royal Box, of course, hears not a thing.

The first official master of ceremonies at a Wembley Final was a Mr Radcliffe. He started conducting 'Abide with Me' for the throng in 1927 (Cardiff 1, Arsenal 0) at the special request, apparently, of Queen Mary. It was, I have read, given a pretty limp and hesitant rendering by the English that day – indeed was not a patch on 'Land of My Fathers' which the Welsh choral societies brought up from Ninian. But the FA continued with the 'tradition'.

A middle-aged, Butlin's redcoat-type, Arthur Caiger, enthusiastically took over, windmilling his arms on the centre-circle podium. He lasted for years, a national institution for a day, but still couldn't get much more than a massed mumbling of a response for the first two lines of Queen Mary's hymn. 'C'mon, let's be havin' you,' he'd bellow. Or 'C'mon, boys and girls, just one more time!' He would always announce himself with 'Testin', testin', testin'.' It was all very village fête parochial.

Mind you, not many took a blind bit of notice. Most got on with chanting increasing and shameless obscenities, or thinking up new lyrics to go with (or against) say, Newcastle's 'Blaydon Races', West Ham's 'Blowing Bubbles', Tottenham's 'Glory Allelujah', or Liverpool's 'You'll Never Walk Alone'.

By Liverpool's run, Mr Caiger had long windmilled his way off over the twin towers and into the sunset. The FA tried to replace him with a number of brave vaudeville artists who did valiant impersonations of such as Bruce Forsyth or Jimmy Tarbuck, but I sense the feeling now is to print the words of 'Abide with Me' in the programme and leave the resulting cacophony up to everyone's conscience.

As long ago as 1959, officialdom had decided to throw in the towel. On April 17 that year *The Times* reported: 'A Wembley Stadium spokesman said on Wednesday that a display by girls of the Coventry Keep Fit Association would take the place, before the Final, of the hymn "Abide with Me".'

Two days later the newspaper printed a letter from the Reverend H. W. R. Elsley:

'Sir – I am the Vicar of the parish in which the Empire Stadium is situated and have been an appreciative guest at Cup Finals for years. I can testify that the hymn has been sung with perfect reverence – but with what amount of understanding is another matter, especially as the words 'fast

118

falls the eventide, the darkness deepens' seem out of place in
broad daylight and sometimes in strong sunshine. It suggests,
too, thoughts of approaching death at all too young an age,
and this sentiment is also out of place on the lips of people
almost all of whom are young and few beyond middle age. Yrs
etc . . .'

By April 26, a week before the match, the hymn was
reprieved – though I cannot think where to check whether the
Coventry muscle molls made it to the metropolitan maypole
or not.

By the way, that 1959 Final (Nottingham Forest 2, Luton
1) was watched by a sprog called Reg Dwight. His uncle,
Forest's right winger, Roy Dwight, had been transferred from
Fulham the year before. Eight minutes after the start at
Wembley he scored Forest's first. Half-an-hour later he was
carried off the pitch with a broken leg. The boy who was there
to watch his uncle fall that day is now called Elton John.

You never know, Watford and their chairman might just
have got the old stadium on harmonious song. Well, they had
something to squawk about – even though they lost to

Everton. In their 86-year-old history, Watford AFC have only known of Wembley as a station ten stops down the Metropolitan Line. Nor is friend Elton their first showbiz star. The club have a tradition in light entertainment. In the 1920s, before they moved to their Vicarage Road pitch, the club played at the West Herts Rugby Club in Cassio Road. I quote from the classic *Football Grounds of England & Wales* by Simon Inglis, who in turn acknowledges he cribbed from Oliver Phillips' comprehensive Watford history: before one Cassio Road match, 'a local character called Joey Goodchild performed his usual trick of climbing onto the grandstand roof to perform a tapdance for the delight of the crowd. But on this occasion someone asked him to stop, and he fell off the roof and landed on a gentleman, whose glasses were broken, and an unfortunate lady. She received £25 compensation from the club, and Joey's dancing had to come to an end.'

So, if you had scanned the rim round Wembley's corrugated, cantilevered grandstands on Cup Final day, up there, as Elton shielded his spectacles, might just have been the grinning ghost of Joey Goodchild, swaying his hips and tap-tap-tapdancing to the hymns and arias. It would have matched any display by the Coventry Keep Fit Association – and have livened up 'Abide With Me', I'm telling you.

MIXED BAG

Name Dropping

I spent a day with Jackie Stewart, the former motor racing ace, at his sumptuous home above Lake Geneva. At lunch the subject of childhood heroes came up, and between pudding and coffee Jackie was away upstairs rummaging in his attic – to come down triumphantly with a battered, old autograph book.

It had been his most treasured possession – more so even than his first set of spanners – back in the 1950s when he was an apprentice garage mechanic in Dumbartonshire and had occasionally travelled with his elder brother, Jimmy, to the racetracks down south. There they all were . . . squiggles of Hawthorn, Ascari, Farina, Brooks, and – still Stewart's most coveted – Stirling Moss.

Are today's kids still at it? 'Sign here, please, Mister?' Or has the adventure, let alone the simple, wide-eyed romance, gone out of sport for a generation weaned on the inane, so-called intimacies of television after-match quotes, or meaningless newspaper confessions? If the 1930s were for cigarette cards, my 40s and 50s were for autograph collecting. What do they collect now? Anyway, I suppose one Henry Kelly is worth ten Henry Coopers.

The first autograph I 'collected' was Charlie Barnett's. He was Gloucestershire's opening bat – and once completed a corking century for England at Trent Bridge by rattling the first ball after lunch to the pickets for four. He hit as fiercely as he looked down on us local oiks. He owned wet-fish shops in

Cirencester and Cheltenham and rode with the Beaufort and Berkeley foxhounds. He lived at Chalford, near Stroud, and one day a friend and I rode our bicycles up the winding Cotswold hill and lay in wait with our brand new autograph books. He came neither in nor out, and we were far too scared to knock boldly on the front door. Then I had a brainwave. Charlie's daughter, Judy, was at the local convent school, in the same class as my sister. A modest bribe was negotiated and, lo and behold, a couple of days later, the book came back with Page One inscribed 'Best of luck, Francis – C. J. Barnett'.

It was cheating. But I was off. That was the early summer of 1947 and by the end of August's Cheltenham Festival I had the whole of the Gloucester team and quite a few of the 'visitors' too. Most valued of those was 'W. J. Edrich', and when, two years later, I nabbed the amiable, scatty sig. 'Denis Compton', on the same page, I headed it in my wayward, juvenile capitals 'THE MIDDLE SEX TWINS', making two words out of the London county in an unknowing, but interesting, Freudian slip.

My big coup of 1948 was to get the Australians. I simply sent my book to the Visitor's Dressing Room at Worcester at the end of April, marked 'For the attention of Mr Donald Bradman'. Back came a sheet of paper, on which all of them had written their names. It remains, perhaps, the finest side ever to tour. I breakfasted that morning in heaven.

Many years later the cricket historian, David Frith, warned me about second-hand signatures. He said he once knew a pre-war Aussie Test player who had been lumbered with a thousand autograph sheets on the boat coming over and to prove it had reeled-off for him a near-perfect Bradman, O'Reilly and Oldfield!

I suspected none of that in 1948. Wretchedly and alas, I have lost that old, beloved autograph book in the general jetsam of moving on, but I can still close my eyes and recall The Don's neat little, joined-together writing, 'D. G. Bradman'. If I keep them closed, I could still do you a passable forgery of the upright, well schooled 'W. A. Brown' or the cack-handed 'A. R. Morris' or his lefty apprentice, R. N. Harvey'. I drooled over them and I learned them almost by heart: 'C. McCool' was the most juvenile and unstylish of handwriting, and 'W. A. Johnston' and 'D. Ring' the most confusing couple of scrawls. You had to work those two out by a process of elimination. The two wicketkeepers, 'D. Tallon' and 'R. A. Saggers' were straightforward and standing up. 'R. A. Hamence' was schoolmasterly, well formed and correct.

Sid Barnes, cobber, and clobbering opening bat plus suicide-point fielder, was the only one to 'sign' his name with a rubber-stamp – 'S. G. Barnes' bashed out from an exciting, tearaway's, purply-coloured inkpad. The mesmerizing Miller signed just as the legend said he did – writing a very readable, sub-copperplate 'eith ille', and then adding the capitals, 'K' and 'M', with a gorgeous and flowery flourish.

That stuck-in sheet remained the highspot of my collection. I kept it going for another ten years or so. I had T. E. Bailey before he started writing 'Trevor' as his prefix, and likewise D. B. Close before he was 'Brian'. I got Tommy Lawton from soccer, and Dai Dower from boxing. I had a genuine Billy Wright, too – in person one evening when he opened a local soccer ground. I knew by then that the boaster's knack was to have approached them personally, not to write enclosing your book and the old s.a.e.

Once, at school, I stole from a friend's desk (just to own for a morning, and look, honest!) a piece of paper bearing the signature of a Cheshire dentist who that summer had played for England at cricket. It had been, temptingly, in an envelope marked 'Lancs CCC'.

This prep school was in the habit of having snap personal checks and searches whenever it happened to take the fancy of suspicious Benedictine monk teachers. Suddenly, that very morning, they announced a turnout of desks and pockets. Wherever we were, we had to freeze and wait for these ancient suss laws to be enacted. The stolen, valued, piece of paper was in my pocket. Briefly, I panicked. Then I did the only thing a hoodlum could do. Uneasy, but still unsuspected, I transferred the stolen piece of paper from pocket to hand; then I coughed and sneezed to create an innocent's disturbance as the fuzz approached; they were unaware that at the same time as I was snuffling, was popping the guilty thing into my

125

mouth. I am the only man I know to have actually eaten the signature of 'K. Cranston (Lancs & England)'.

I suppose I've become more cynical since, when Gloucestershire played a few county matches at Stroud, I daringly asked 'B. D. Wells' to add his much loved nickname to his autograph in my book – and he did, with a smile and a snappy line in inverted commas: 'Best regards, *The Bomber*'.

Esther Rantzen might have made an important point when she once said, 'I don't know why these autograph-hunters don't just forge them: no-one would ever know.'

At Gloucester Wagon Works ground, Fred Trueman once lined up all us kids. The queue was as long as an M4 'tailback' in today's holiday season. Trueman asked each of us our name before planting that personalized, and hugely treasured, set of initials in our book – 'To Francis, from F.S.T.'. Yet, over a quarter of a century later, on the radio, Fred was sneering the other day at those faithful signature-sentries who have ever followed him. 'I dunno,' he said, 'men keep comin' up an' sayin' they want my autograph f'their nephew. I tell them blunt: if y'want me signature f'your nephew, then I'll get me own newphew t'sign the ruddy thing.'

Not the sort of thing we pleading, shaking, quaking autograph-hunters want to hear. Fred never toured India with England. Tony Lewis did, as captain in 1972. He was a marvellously civil, genteel, humorous and much-loved leader. In India you have to be; they worship cricket. Five hundred autographs a day is the norm even for a visiting net bowler. Lewis would sign his name into the night. One day, at Bangalore or Kanpur, or wherever, a man knocked on his door each hour of the day prior to the Test Match – 'My dear uncle, Lewis-sahib, please sign these sheets of paper for my big and beloved family!'

Tony would readily and dutifully sign each proffered piece 'A. R. Lewis'. By the second day of the Test, a gateman at last felt himself duty-bound to approach the England captain. Surely he had been too profligate with his invitations. Every sheet Tony had signed had been topped and tailed with the typewritten legend 'Please admit to Test Match. Signed, A. R. Lewis, Captain of England'.

The greats sign. I have seldom known Jack Nicklaus, Bjorn

Borg, Pele or, if you plot the course to a quiet corner, Lester Piggott, refuse to sign an autograph. The most ready, and willing, and friendly signer of anyone I have observed over the years is the boxer, Muhammad Ali. He would go out of his way, even rip pages from spivvy autograph books to sign and give to kids in the queue who only had cigarette packets to offer.

Once, before some faraway fight, I asked him to sign a programme for my twelve-year-old nephew. 'Put "To Mark, Keep punching, Yrs Ali",' I asked, and the great man duly did, although he was going into the ring within minutes.

I sent it off proudly by airmail. When I got home, I asked to see the famous signature. Said Mark's father: 'I'm sorry you asked about that. I'm afraid he swopped it last week – for two Lou Macaris!'

Writing Wrongs

Once upon a time, sportswriting was simply a matter of knowing what hat to wear – and not to mix your drinks till you had noted which team had kicked off with a rush. Now we are expected to observe terrace hooligans as if we were the social services' correspondent, add up earnings and prize-money with the smarmy smoothness of the pinstripers on the city pages, and burrow into *Hansard* instead of *Wisden* to sniff the drift of the latest sport 'n' politics hooha.

With hats and booze it was all a cinch. Your exes could cover, with profit, the necessary variety of headgear you had to have hanging on the old antelope antlers in the hall. You needed the topper to raise at Ascot as well as the lovaty-brown, flat, checked job, peak for the touching of, for Sandown and Cheltenham. On Wimbledon mornings you could take your pick, trying on a variety: should it be the battered old straw job; or the Frew Macmillan autographed canvas cap; or the lumpen, linen, pudding-basin thing patented by Papa McEnroe; or his son's headband with a feather rampant at the rear; or even the lovely, long-ago, green perspex eyeshade of Louise Brough?

Henley was always jolly boater weather, and at cricket, except in the Lord's pavilion where you weren't allowed anyway, the snotted, knotted, spotted red hankie sunhat was allowed to pass muster anywhere. At golf, too, anything went, from an ear-muffed 'Sherlock' to those catchpenny titfers which you clamp to your crown and open up like a baby umbrella: they usually bore such legends as 'You're All Right, Jack!' or 'Go Get 'Em, Arnie!'

Selection of refreshment was an even easier matter. Sporting writers drank beer, chased, on special occasions and anniversaries like the chiming of the hour, with a tumblerful of Scotch whisky. At some events, and when, say, researching a colour piece at Henley, Wimbledon or Ascot, your expenses would readily stand you the odd tankard of Pimms or Plymouth Pink. The Bollinger tent at the British Open, for instance, has always been a necessary vantage point from which to study the perfection of Trevino's technique with a five iron into a swirling, Scottish, seaside gale.

Even ringsiders need refreshment. After his stint as a poet of pugilism, Norman Mailer remarked: 'The popular assumption that professional boxers do not have brains comes from sportswriters, but then sportswriters' brains are themselves damaged by the obligation to be clever every day. And the quantities of booze necessary to lubricate such racing of the mental gears ends up giving sportswriters the equivalent of a good many punches to the head.'

It has all changed. Sport-hackery demands these days that we pack a bowler hat and carry a brolly rolled into a spear. We must drink afternoon tea with sources close to foreign governments. We must do the doorstepping for diplomatic corps. And prime the political pundits. At the Olympic Games in Moscow, stopwatches were stopped and vodka remained corked: we were all sober-sided experts in Afghanistan. In New Zealand we rugger-buggers on the trail of the Lions were not beery-breathed experts in lineout play; we were financial reporters, speculating for the city pages on how much Ollie Campbell would be worth if he was asked to join an Australian's professional circus.

No athlete can draw breath now without us encircling him, pencils poised, to enquire about his attitude to those twin roots of evil – money and South Africa. Oh, for the not so distant day we asked the chairman of the England cricket selectors, Alec Bedser, how, when we were thrown out of Guyana at the end of the 'Jackman Affair', he interpreted the Gleneagles Convention. The old boy sniffed the air suspiciously. 'Gleneagles?' he said. 'What's a golf course got to do with it?'

A sporting wordsmith's world has changed in just fifteen years. In the Paris riots of 1968 an English rugby league team found itself 'trapped' in the capital. They were accompanied by one sportswriter. For a day or two just about all communications with the outside world were severed: phones didn't work and airports were closed. The doughty old Northerner, unaware that anything was up, spent that Sunday ceaselessly trying to raise his Manchester office from the telephone kiosk in the reception hall of his hotel. His deadline had almost passed. At last his perseverance paid off and, miraculously, he got through. He was connected at once to the news editor. 'Well done, Albert! Brilliant! We can't get anyone in. What's happening?'

'Well,' said Albert in his stately, slow, Lancysheer accent, 'it's queer place this. Very excitable folk. Why, a tank 'as just crashed through into front lobby 'ere as I'm talking t'you . . .

''Fantastic!' interrupted the news editor, 'I'll put you straight through to a copy typist. And let it run, old boy. Give us the lot!'

'I haven't got all that much,' said Albert.

'Well, just give us as much as you can – anything off the top of your head – and we'll dress it up something wonderful this end! There's a big bonus in this for you, Albert, don't forget that. Let it sing, old boy. Anything you can think of.'

Jubilantly, he connected Albert to the copytakers, and whoopingly started rejigging his whole front page. Albert started dictating, precisely and ponderously – 'Eric Jenkinson, the Widnes prop forward, will have a fitness test on this suspect left knee tomorrow morning prior to being included in the team to play Paris on Wednesday . . .'

A couple of hundred more words in similar vein and, his job well done, he hung up and, with scarce a glance at the foyer rubble, he trudged upstairs. What a nice guy that news editor was, he thought, as he lay on his bed for one last flip through his saucy French magazine – prior to donning his old brown, Eddie Waring-type trilby, and wandering out to get pissed on a few Pernods down the Pigalle.

Pay Up and Play

Money is how they keep the score in bigtime sport these days. Sport is business now and well, business is business.

It's nothing really new, mind you – Kid Cain would not have put his title on the line against Boy Abel if the money hadn't been right – it's only that it is all out in the open now and backhanders cannot possibly match the trumpeted upfront money, money, money. Like the jilted television entrepreneur, Mr Kerry Packer, said in 1977: 'C'mon, we are all harlots. It is all a matter of price. How much do you fellows want?'

Is anything left that is unloved by lucre? Even the Boat Race, Gawd help us, is sponsored. We have to call the 'Varsity Rugby Match the 'Bowring Trophy' now. The FA Cup is still the FA Cup, thank heavens, but for how long? Wimbledon has hocked itself to sponsors to such an extent that any day now we'll be having to call it the Robinson's Barley Classic, or whatever. The day before the century-old, annual England v Wales rugger fixture in 1982 I received in the post an order from some public relations twerp demanding that I refer to the match in future as *The British Telecom Challenge*.

At teatime on the first Saturday of the new football season, I switched on the radio. The old winter-warming tune burst forth. *Dadum-dadum-dadum-dadum-da-diddleydum-da-da*. 'Good evening,' the man said in his po-voiced manner that still cannot disguise from the first syllable that it's a home, away or draw – 'Good evening,' he said. 'Here are the *Canon* League Football Results.' Bless us and save us.

English League soccer is promoting Canon UK, a Japanese photographic company. A number of individual League clubs are already sponsored by Japanese firms. It might be fun – very briefly – when Sanyo United meet Hitachi Gunners under the banner of Canon. As David Lacey, the *Guardian*'s waspish and worldly-wise football writer, sighed the other day: 'All those Nipponese giants battling it out thinly disguised as footballers; the *Seven Samurai* remade, wardrobe by Addidas.'

The Football League have even been bribed to bung their legendary and traditional old Championship Trophy – admittedly a bit of an Edwardian silversmith's follly – into the attic and accept a smart new bauble from the commissioning Japs. As Lacey said, 'The winners will presumably be expected to fill the new cup with saki, and eat with seaweed'.

And what if Canon don't sell any more cameras? What if ye traditional UK soccer hooligan starts to offend ye traditional sensibilities of courteous, honourable Japanese businessman? What if Canon get a new chairman who prefers, say, opera to soccer? Then the Football League will be sniffing around for a new title, a new trophy. Remember the Rothmans-Berger-Servowarm Isthmian League a couple of years ago? Did you know that in Ireland they are having to call their century-old club championship the *Kentucky Fried Chicken Irish League?* Fingerlickin' horrors.

Sport can backfire on sponsors. During Don Revie's disastrous stewardship of the England football team in the middle of the 1970s, he did a deal with the sports outfitters, Admiral, and after two games I remember Michael Parkinson observing: 'If I were managing director of Admiral I would be looking for a get-out clause in the contract before Mr Revie's wonders can do my product any more damage.'

On the whole, I would guess, sport has made more for the player than the punter. Peter de Savary, for instance, might have lost six million pounds indulging in his hobby at the America's Cup yacht race, but his jack tars have been pretty jolly over their win-or-lose wages. Another team 'owner', Rudy Carpenter, of the Philadelphia Phillies once said 'I'm going to write a book, *How to make a Small Fortune in Sport*. You start with a large fortune.'

In America, the salaries paid to even run-of-the-mill 'midfielders' at the leading football, baseball or ice hockey clubs are astronomical. They have ruined many a millionaire owner. When the wise-cracking US impressario, Ted Turner, had to sell his star player, Andy Messersmith, to the New York Yankees in order to bale out his Atlanta Braves, he observed: 'He had to go. For $300,000 a year Andy wouldn't even say "Hello". He tried to give the impression he was smarter than I am. Come to think of it, I suppose he was right. I was so dumb that I gave him the contract in the first place.'

When the ruthless Bill Veeck took over another US team a few years ago, he warned: 'I want the fans to know that the White Sox management will scheme, connive, steal, and do everything possible to win the Championship pennant . . . except pay increased salaries.'

Before the Americans beat the Russians in that sensational – and officially amateur – ice hockey game at the 1980 Winter Olympics, Harold Ballard, of the Toronto Maple Leafs, summed up the rewards on offer: 'If the Russkies win they go home and find better conditions in their house, like two electric light bulbs instead of one. If the Americans win, it makes no difference at all for at a very minimum Hockey League wage you are making fifty grand before you even get started.'

In the old days – when 'sponsors' more often than not were a shady 'syndicate' – sportsmen had to work a little harder. When Joe Louis thrashed Max Baer in 1935 at the Yankee Stadium, Maxie reckoned he earned every bit of his $100,000. The Brown Bomber floored him twice in the third, and then in the fourth Max softly genuflected on one knee and stayed there till the toll of ten. He then rose, shook hands with his assailant, and ambled off to his corner to collect his little brown envelope, explaining 'Sure I quit. He hit me eighteen times while I was in the act of falling that last time. I don't intend to be cutting up paper dolls for a livelihood. Besides I gotta wife and family to think about. If anyone wants to see the execution of Maxie Baer he's gotta pay more than twenty-five dollars for a ringside seat!'

134

Though legitimate sponsors now queue up to milk everything from a boxing occasion – except of course to get hit on the nose – the leading fighters stil hope to keep their wallet fat. Not many succeed. Last month when I was in America I noticed that they were selling videos of Muhammad Ali's fight with Leon Spinks for twenty dollars. Leon has fallen on hard times already and, said someone, 'Christ! For that money, Spinks will come to your house!'

Money, money, money . . . even in richly sponsored sport it goes in one pocket and out the other. Like Ilie Nastase said when mentioning that he forgot to report the loss of his American Express card: 'Whoever stole it is bound to be spending less than my wife.'

Muscular Muse

I enjoyed the recent competition on sporting verse. And worse. It was inspired by the welcome news that a London publisher, Junction Books, is preparing an anthology. I wonder how wide and deep they are trawling. New poems for old? Will the editors just rejig the old orders – a touch of Thompson, some Arlott and Abse and Oakes, Ross and Robertson-Glasgow? Or are they planning to come over and stand on the terraces with the rest of us?

No offence to that lot, of course. Alan Ross, particularly, has written some outstanding stuff on cricket and soccer. Even my haphazard learning can recite a snatch of his homage to Stanley Matthews:

> *Horseless, though jockey-like and jaunty,*
> *Straddling the touchline, live margin*
> *Not out of the game, nor quite in . . .*

Or even his own boyhood afternoons, at prep school in the autumn term:

> *Studs and mud, the memorable dribble,*
> *Rhododendrons at the back of the net.*

Yet that last line's the giveaway to make my point. John Toshack, of Cardiff City, Liverpool and Swansea City, never played in front of a rhododendroned Kop, but he is the only leading sportsman I have come across to have attempted a slim autobiography in verse. It was called *Gosh it's Tosh!* and went, as they say, something like this:

> *Ray Clemence kicks a long high ball,*
> *And Barcelona are about to fall.*
> *For Kevin Keegan wins the race,*
> *And flicks it on into a space.*
> *By my right foot the ball is met,*
> *And in a flash it's in the net!!*

It sold thousands, and jolly good luck to him. Actually, another top pro, from Toshack's time, is also a poet. John Farmer, Stoke City's goalkeeper and an England Under-23 international under Alf Ramsey. At seventeen, in his first precocious season, he saved a penalty from Jimmy Greaves. Then came Banks from Leicester to Stoke. Then came Shilton. Then Banks again. John languished as reserve gloveman. Then Banks lost an eye in an accident. Farmer was in again – and wrote 'To Gordon Banks. On the coming of my Second Career after his accident':

> *Your magic moments of inspiration*
> *Will serve me well*
> *For in the cheers and in the air*
> *I now much breathe*
> *Your winding spell will never fade*
> *Or die*
> *And my hands that once were frozen*
> *Are thawing fast.*

That and a hundred other poignant, dog-eared poems plopped on my dormat one morning in the 1970s. The polo-necked romantic. But no snazzy publisher wanted second XI thoughts. I wonder if Junction Books have contacted John Farmer?

One nice soccer snatch I memorized some dozen years ago

137

was Martin Hall's Black Country lament:

> *The night Stan Cullis got the sack*
> *Wolverhampton wandered round in*
> *   circles*
> *Like a disallowed goal*
> *Looking for a friendly linesman.*

Tosh notwithstanding, Liverpool continues to have a go. Of course, the red and the blue makes for a mix an' a match. Roger McGough once wrote touchingly of the singular Scouse who couldn't decide on his loyalty:

> *I'd be bisexual if I had time for sex*
> *Cos its Goodison one week and Anfield the next.*

Rather like the song I heard the other day, sung by a Liverpool folk singer, Bridie. She called it *Romeo an' Juliet*, 'cos:

> *Juliet's dad was Everton mad*
> *While Romeo's da was a Shankly lad.*

There have been reams on hunting an' fishing, but what about cycling and snooker and darts? James Kirkup has written at least one poem on Rugby League, and Roy McFadden, too, on a Rugby Union international:

> *Crumpled packs dishevel the holy ground,*
> *While fledgling wings inch forward for a sign.*
> *In forced tumescent waves the faceless crowd*
> *Washes the field in sublimating sound;*
> *Implores, deplores, ejaculates aloud.*
> *On, up and under, forwards. Charge the line.*

Gavin Ewart has written some good sports poems, as tricksy, yet as direct as a run by Finney. Brian Glanville, too. But I wonder if Junction Books have sought out Mrs E. K., of Northampton, whose teenage son was soccer mad and would one day play at Wembley. She sent me this, saying she was nearly a Wembley mother but:

> *Now it will never be;*
> *Perhaps because of Wembley itself.*
> *An image in the mind of the boy,*
> *Having a reality more tangible*
> *Than life itself.*
> *Was it because of this?*
> *Did the road turn green*
> *And the noise of the cars*
> *Become the cheers of the crowd?*
> *I hope he was scoring the winning goal*
> *At the moment of impact.*

I wonder if Junction have stopped off at Anthony Lias? There have been, as I say, some marvellously evocative cricket poems over the century, but the occasional times Lias has turned over an arm shows he's up there with the best. In his *Presence of Lions* there is his fast bowler's gathering run-up, and:

> *the wind that ruffles his shirt has entered him.*

Lighter, I like the time Lias turned up to his Shropshire village match to renew his annual bat-ball battle with the opposition's veteran, grey-haired, horny-handed, demon bowler. But the old boy had died, 'in harness', the week before:

> *When skipper handed Charlie the new ball,*
> *That end was taken care of for the day;*
> *Charlie'd grin boyishly, then wheel away*
> *Until he'd snapped up six, or eight, or all.*
> *This once, however, Charlie couldn't scoff*
> *So lightly at his sixty years and odd;*
> *For halfway through his umpteenth over, God*
> *Overruled skipper and took Charlie off.*

Ahh!

Mixed Doubles

The death of Johnny Arnold in a Southampton hospital lops another name from the short, short, list of double internationals who played for England at both cricket and soccer. Now only Willie Watson and Arthur Milton are alive to tell their tales. Willie, in his mid-sixties, lives in South Africa. Arthur is a postman in Bristol.

I *think* this makes up the full list: Alfred Lyttelton, William Gunn, L. H. Gay, R. E. Forster, C. B. Fry, J. Sharp, H. Makepeace, H. T. W. Hardinge, and A. Ducat. In the wartime 'Victory' internationals, Patsy Hendren and Denis Compton also won soccer caps. Now, with soccer's frenzies eroding every summer, it is hard enough to find even a League footballer finding time for cricket, and men like Chris Balderstone (Carlisle United and Leicestershire), Phil Neale (Lincoln City and Worcestershire), and even Ian Botham (Scunthorpe and Somerset) are already sporting anachronisms. Why, you get the feeling these days that some Football League clubs are even loath to release their men to play *soccer* for England!

With a romantic's timing, dear old Johnny Arnold died in the very week of the April changeover, the penultimate week of winter when in those expectant springs of long ago he would bung his football boots into his London landlady's cupboard and hot-foot it to Waterloo to catch the Southern Belle and hurry to pad up for the nets at Hampshire's County Ground. He played 200 games on the left wing for Fulham (and half as many again for Southampton) and scored 21,000 runs for Hampshire. He was chosen once for England at cricket (a duck and 34 against New Zealand at Lord's in 1931) and once at soccer, against Scotland at Hampden two years later.

Arnold started his long 'double' career just as Andy Ducat was ending his. Ducat, whose friends called him 'Mac', scored 23,000 for Surrey, though he failed in his one Test against Australia in 1921. His six soccer caps bridged the First War. He died at the wicket, bat in hand, in a match at Lord's in 1942 between the Surrey and Sussex Home Guard XIs. *Wisden* records: 'He began his innings before lunch and was 17 at the interval. On resuming he scored steadily, then he hit a ball from Eaton to mid-on; the ball was returned to the bowler, who was about to send down the next delivery when Ducat fell forward and apparently died immediately.' The match was abandoned. In its tabulated scorecard, *Wisden*, usually the fount of all truth, wrote, 'Private A. Ducat . . . not out 29,' instead of the possibly correct 'retired dead 29'. As Benny Green noted in his whopping anthology of the great Almanack: 'Ducat is one of the very few sporting figures in English history of whom it could be said that the next ball was literally his dying thought.'

When Ducat died Willie Watson, though away at the war, was already on the books of Yorkshire CCC and Sunderland AFC. He won six soccer caps for England in the 1950s as one of that long gone breed, 'the cultured wing-half'. His main job for those stars in stripes at Roker was as straight man and feed for the relentless, crackling genius of Len Shackleton. He played in twenty-three cricket Tests as a lefthanded No. 5, and his most glorious hour – or, rather six hours – was in 1953 when he batted all day with Trevor Bailey at Lord's to thwart Lindwall and Miller and a seemingly certain Australian victory.

Incidentally, Bailey himself was not half a bad footballer. The game also provided him with his now universal nickname, 'The Boil'. Doug Insole, another England cricketer, started it when the two Cambridge double blues were on a soccer tour of Switzerland with, I think, Dulwich Hamlet. A Swiss spectator kept shouting, in pidgin English: 'C'mon *Boiley*, get rid of it!' or cuckoo-clock words to that effect.

Denis Compton might not have played in a *full* peacetime international, but like Ducat (with Aston Villa in 1926) he won an FA Cupwinner's medal with Arsenal in 1950. C. B. Fry, by the way, missed out, getting a loser's medal with Southampton in 1902, where reports said, 'The one weakness of his game was the usual amateur's fault of heading with hunched shoulders.'

Two years later, Compton's place as wingman for the Gunners had been taken by Arthur Milton, who in twenty-six summers was also to score over 32,000 runs for Gloucestershire, hold 759 catches, and score a century in the first of his six Test Matches. In 1952, after just a dozen first-team games for Arsenal, he was picked for England against the Austrians at Wembley.

Arthur remembers: 'I didn't play very well. At Arsenal I had little Jimmy Logie lining up glorious passes for me to run up to. For England my inside-right was Ivor Broadis and he didn't have a good game. Billy Wright was my half-back and he was one-footed on his right so kept slinging out passes to the left to Bailey and Medley. Within half an hour I had vanished from the match, and was too inexperienced to get back.' He was never chosen again.

I still see Arthur sometimes when I go back to the West, or when he is persuaded to turn out for a charity cricket match. The old hero is still slim, still diffident, still casual, still slightly stooping on his bow legs. But he says he has never been happier than now as a postman; he is up at five rain or shine, whistling an accompaniment daily to the dawn chorus on his old British Telecom regulation boneshaker, his sack up-front in the basket. The Clifton Downs are his early morning beat.

Arthur shakes his head and smiles contentedly when his mates in the sorting office say to him, 'Art, you could have made a fortune if you was playing sport today.' His Arsenal contract gave him £8.10s a week, his first at cricket came to £200 for the season. He gets on with his 'street order' sorting. 'It's just a different game now', he tells them.

Sure is. For Arthur Milton is the last of the vanishing line. Simply, there will never again be a double England international at soccer and cricket. Ever.

Black Power

Since 1972 the strides made by Britain's multi-racial society in sport have been sensational. I covered two Olympic Games in the 1960s and, offhand, I cannot recall the British having any but all-white teams. I remember, of course, that electric sprinter, Marilyn Neufville, of the Cambridge Harriers in south-east London, but when it came to the 1970 Commonwealth Games she chose to run for Jamaica – she won and broke the world record.

Then, of a sudden in the mid-1970s, came the explosion – and dashing young smilers with lovely names like Ainsley and Daley, Verona, Tessa and Fatima were running, jumping and seldom standing still. The playing fields of England were helping cure those inner city blues.

There had been pioneers prepared to put up with the prejudice. In the First World War, the Germans had interned a native of British Guiana, Harry Edward. I can discover no reason why he found himself there in the first place, but on his release he settled in England. Friends who noticed he never missed a bus persuaded him to enter the Amateur Athletic Association championships at the White City. For several following summers no-one could get near him, indeed he remains to this day the only man to have won three AAA titles – on the same afternoon – at 100, 220 and 440 yards.

Also from British Guiana – his parents brought him over on a banana boat when he was six months old – was Jack London. In 1928, as a medical student – 'Doctor London of

London', he would introduce himself – he was chosen to compete in the Amsterdam Olympics. He broke the 100 metres record in his semi-final but was beaten into second place in the decider – then strolled across to give it a go at the high-jump pit.

After the next war there was Arthur Wint and Emmanuel McDonald Bailey. Both had served in the RAF. Wint won the 440 yards Olympic title in 1948 and later became the Jamaican High Commissioner in London. Bailey was a boyhood hero of mine, and I suppose the first black man who crept into the consciousness of our faraway village in the warm and cuddly West of England. One of the first pictures I stuck in my scrapbook was of the finish of the 100 yards in those Wembley Olympics. Remember? When every picture told a story, not gave you an arty close-up of a panting nostril or whirring, out-of-focus ankle. Dillard, La Beach, Patton, McQuorquodale and Co. . . . McDonald Bailey was last, and the nation sighed for their adopted Trinidadian.

Two winters ago I was in Port-of-Spain and, to escape a sudden shower, ducked into a cheery little sidestreet cafe called The Talipot. I got talking to the owner and waiter, a black man with grey hair, a gleaming smile, slim as a stick and as fit as a flea. It turned out to be McDonald Bailey. Enchanted, I told him about my scrapbook picture. 'Disappointed? Oh, no, not at all. Just making the final was a triumph in itself. Three weeks before the Games, my thigh went. With ten days left, I got an abscess under my arm. Four days to go and, would you believe, I got laryngitis! Yep, I suppose it was all psychological – though no-one knew anything about such things in those days!' And the charming man laughed fit to bust.

Actually, the first recorded evidence I can trace of a black British athlete was the first man in Britain ever to run 100 yards in even time (ten seconds dead) under championship conditions. He was a Jamaican, Arthur Wharton, who won the AA title at Stamford Bridge in 1886 and later kept goal for Preston North End.

Soccer, like athletics, has seen a warming revolution in these matters over the last decade. If Wharton was the first black pro footballer, he was followed by Walter Tull, who

145

came up from one of the Kentish ports and played seven games for Tottenham Hotspur in 1909 before he was transferred to Northampton Town. 'Enthusiasts will throng to see him,' forecast the *Northants Telegraph*, as it described him as 'a trickster of an inside-forward'.

Later, there was Lindy Delaphenha, who played in Portsmouth's Championship team of 1946, and remember the stir it caused on the front pages when Leeds United played two coloured men, Albert Johanneson and Jerry Francis, against Stoke City in 1961. And Charlie Williams, who used to wow them on the wing at Barnsley and later became a well-known black (and blue) comedian.

Until the 1980s – and it is unusual now for the England soccer team to take the field without one or two black players – I suppose the most successful black footballer was Johnny 'Jack' Leslie, who scored 134 goals for Plymouth Argyle in the Twenties. Many thought him the best inside-forward in the land. Brian Woolnough's enlightenng book *Black Magic* quotes the old man who, in his eighties, was boot-boy and general factotum in the West Ham United dressing room: 'My manager, Bob Jack, called me in one day and made me so happy. "Johnny," he said, "you have been picked to play for England!" Then he embraced me.' But when the team was officially released, he was not in it. "At first they must have forgot I was a coloured boy," he recalled sadly.'

Alas, there's still a bit of it about, and it is sickening sometimes on a Saturday afternoon to hear visiting players being booed just because they are black. The yobs of the National Front must surely tire of it soon. As the graffiti had it at Wembley the night before Luther Blissett, then of Watford, scored a hatful of goals for England a couple of years ago:

> *It's niggers this and niggers that*
> *And send the bastards back*
> *But when Luther scores for England*
> *It'll be Wave the Union Jack.*

Good Sports

It is appropriate that the very year the historic, and hitherto self-sufficient, English Football League sold itself to a sponsor should coincide with three notable amateur centenaries. In 1883 an amateur team last contested the FA Cup Final – Old Etonians losing 1–2 to Blackburn Olympic. In the same year Corinthian Casuals FC completed their first season. And 1983 saw the hundredth university match between Oxford and Cambridge.

What, I wonder, would those grand and casual old Corinthians, 'Pa' Jackson, C. B. Fry and G. O. Smith, have made of the sight of England's current hair-permed professional foulers nipponing about the midfield in aid of the Canon Photographic company from the land of the rising sales graph? Why, even those three would not even take penalty kicks when awarded: it was inconceivable that they would even take the field with chaps who would deliberately commit a foul.

The centenaries are valuable if only to remind today's players and administrators and enthusiasts that their game is rooted in the absolute moral philosophies of Christian sportsmanship. In 1955, C. B. Fry wrote a foreword to Edward Grayson's valuable history, *Corinthian-Casuals and Cricketers*, which has recently and rewardingly been reprinted as a self-evident example, as Grayson says, 'of how *public* sport has moved away from its true nature of fun and playing to the rules since money and politics obtruded'.

The foreword by the estimable Renaissance man – he was at one and the same time the country's best Classics scholar, best No. 3 bat, most promising diplomat, best amateur right full-back, a Master of Wine and the world's longest longjumper – is more timely than when Fry penned it in 1955 at the age of eighty-three: 'There is no doubt that neither football nor cricket would have developed as they have but for the Public Schools. You can tell an audience at Marble Arch, if you like, that the games we now enjoy were developed from the back alleys of London, Birmingham, Leeds or Wigan (all fine cities), but the appeal, although emotional, would not be true to fact.'

When the Old Etonians lost that now historic Cup Final in 1883, they were the Cup holders. The previous year they had beaten Blackburn's other side, the Rovers, by 1–0 at Kennington Oval; but even then the times they were a-changin', for the cotton workers from Lancashire had come down for t'Cup chanting this presumptive victory verse:

> *All hail, ye gallant Rover lads!*
> *Etonians thought you were but cads:*
> *They've found at football game their dads*
> *By meeting Blackburn Rovers.*

The Corinthians were the shop window team for the Public School old boys. On a number of occasions they *were* the England soccer team. G. O. Smith, at centre-forward, was their noblest player. He was an exact contemporary of Fry's – both born in 1872. Smith went to Charterhouse, Fry to Repton. Fry saw all the great centre-fowards of the land from 1888, right up to Dean and Lawton and Charles – he died in 1956, the year Bobby Charlton was baptized a Busby Babe – but always reckoned Smith's 'rating as the finest man in his place who ever played for England is generally accepted . . . clever is not the word: he was inspired'.

When Smith made his first appearance for England against Scotland as an eleventh-hour deputy, *Athletic News* said he was 'a capital forward and a pretty dribbler who lacks shooting power'. Fry pooh-poohs that. 'The yarn that he was weak in the shot in his early first-class seasons is just a yarn. I played often with and against him, and he was as straight and hard a shot as I ever met except perhaps only Steve Bloomer, of Derby County, on one of Steve's better days. GO's was every day'. He swung, adds Fry, 'a marvellously heavy foot', though he was almost frail in build and delicately neat. He also had 'curiously-fine grey eyes and eye-lashes such as any girl would envy.'

Even higher over ye moon were A. Gibson and W. Pickford, who combined in 1906 to write a four-volume treatise, *Association Football and the Men Who Made It*. To them, G.O. was 'a veritable king among athletes. He opposed subtlety to force . . . and when he got hurt – as all men do – he never whined nor grumbled . . . and never funked the biggest back that ever bore down on him. To see him walk quietly onto the field with his hands in his pockets, and watch the fine lines of an intellectual face, one wondered why the student had ventured into the area of football.'

He may have had an intellectual face, but he only managed a Third in History at Oxford's Keble. He became a schoolmaster. Two months before he died – of a stroke in 1943 – Grayson visited the old man at his home in the New Forest. 'Significantly, behind him as we sat, there lay on his couch a newspaper or magazine – I fancy it was an old pre-war copy of *Topical Times* – opened at the page carrying an article with his own photograph and that of Tommy Lawton's great mentor at Everton, "Dixie" Dean. The caption was the old chestnut "Dean or Smith, the Greatest Ever?" He was too wise and modest to be drawn into the controversy; but it was appropriate that my last memory of him should be this span of history – the link between old and new.'

Practice made the professionals more perfect. The casual Corinthians of Smith's time never trained. They just turned up for the match. When the Old Etonians were beaten in the Cup Final of 1883, the pros from Blackburn Olympic had horrified football circles in London by cheerfully admitting they had trained for a week – just as they had when defeating the Old Carthusians at the semi-final.

The *Blackburn Times* of April 7, 1883, lists the occupations of

149

the Olympic team as '3 weavers, a loomer, a gilder, a labourer and a dresser in an iron foundry, a clerk, a plumber, a licensed victualler and a dentist'. The paper noted that the man who owned the local iron foundry, Mr Sydney Yates, had donated one hundred pounds 'towards defraying the heavy costs of preparation for the closing ties of the competition' – which in this case meant the team being able to afford two weeks' full-time training on the sands at Blackpool. In his classic work, *Association Football & English Society, 1863–1915*, Tony Mason mentions that 'much was made of the fact that this Olympic team of northern working men then came south with factory muck still on their brows and conquered the leisure-sated sybarites of Eton'. Yet Mr Yates' 'donation' had given sports sponsorship a first gleam at least in its, as yet unslanted, eye.

I can find no evidence that any penalty was awarded to either side at the Kennington Oval that spring afternoon in 1883. To the amateurs, even getting offside was ungentlemanly. The founder of the Corinthians, N. L. 'Pa' Jackson, wrote in his team orders that 'hanging about on the verge of offside amounted to "sneaking".' He also ruled that 'every allowance should be made for the difficulties that beset a referee, and his decision, even though apparently improper, should be accepted and obeyed without the slightest demur. Silence must be the general rule . . . and if a player get the worst of a charge or of a tussle for the ball, let them admire the skill that has beaten them and let them try to profit by the lesson.'

In those days, as now, the laws of the game insisted a penalty be awarded for any defender's *intentional* offence in the penalty area. The amateurs felt that, by definition, they could only possibly offend *accidentally*, and the award of a penalty kick would besmirch honour and integrity and fair play. Wrote Fry: 'It is a standing insult to have to play under a rule which assumes that players intend to trip, hack and push their opponents, and to behave like cads of the most unscrupulous kidney. I say that the lines marking the penalty area are a disgrace to the playing field.'

When Fry toured South Africa with the Corinthians in 1907, a penalty was awarded against them. Fry ordered his goalkeeper to leave his goal. He had no wish to prevent the other side scoring fairly. Then the Corinthians were awarded a penalty at the other end. The kicker deliberately shot wide of the goal.

How charming it would be – as well a symbolically timely – if the Oxford and Cambridge teams would agree, just for the day and in celebration, to forego the professional foul when they meet in the university match in December.

No – as modern Oxbridge midfield men say these days – *way!*

At The Double

It seems a touch eccentric that during the white-draped, coffin-like days of mid-winter, the first sporting champions to be applauded in Britain in the New Year are *tennis* players. The World Doubles Championships at the Albert Hall.

I fancy most Brits tend to think that, give or take a Davis Cup humiliation or two, serious tennis is played only during that frenzied June fortnight in SW19's old ivied cockpit. In fact throughout the year and the world over, the caravan is rumbling through the forest of greenbacks. Week after week the circus hits town after town. And after the singles come the doubles.

New names lead the parade now, as trippingly rhythmic to tennis buffs as Hobbs and Sutcliffe or Swan and Edgar to others – Taroczy and Gunthardt, Jarryd and Simonsson, Curren and Denton . . . To me, somehow, that trio of teams doesn't yet seem as endurably set in a romantic's dictionary as such old firms as, offhand, McGregor and Sedgman, Mulloy and Patty, Hoad and Rosewall, Smith and Lutz, Newcombe and Roche, Hewitt and Stolle . . . and after Hewitt and Stolle came Hewitt and McMillan. They were my favourites of all time. Hewitt, fierce and broad and bald and temperamental, a grizzly old bear who growled; McMillan, tidy, trim, unfussy, almost faceless under his baggy white cap. Darby and Joan, they were together for almost twenty years. When they went on court of an early evening the Wimbledon player's tearoom would empty, and those late for a seat on the Centre would sit in a silent, admiring throng around the television sets.

Arthur Ashe once confided about the greatness of Hewmac: 'If you saw those two old guys practising on a court somewhere and didn't know who they were, you'd think anyone on your block could beat them. But you've gotta believe it, that bald guy with the paunch and the skinny kid with the cap can beat anyone. They look like a pick-up father-and-son team but they can beat anyone on the whole planet earth.'

Hewitt's right hand wielded a massive carpet-beater, but he used it with a surprising delicacy; he was a dabbing and dinking pokerwork player, a swordsman at the net who would slice and nick and cut away till the far side of the court was covered in blood. McMillan cut most of the swathes round the baseline; I think he was the first player I saw with the two-handed grip; his forehand was like he was fishing for a big one in a choppy sea; and if Hewitt didn't get them, Mac's unflappy, inch-perfect goemetry would bludgeon the opposition to death. The Head and the Hat.

As they worked the net as one, the sheer instincts and anticipations of these two elasticated Siamese twins were awesome. You couldn't often catch them in worried consultation. Their signals seemed telepathic. Watch at the Albert Hall how some doubles teams use elaborate finger signals behind the back. For instance, the man at the net might scratch his left buttock, or show his server crossed fingers to indicate he intends to poach the first cross-court return, or perhaps clench his fist to mean he will only take something down the line; or three fingers in the small of the back might mean that as soon as the service passes his ear on the outward journey he will move back to the baseline pronto.

Of course, one mustn't forget *mixed* doubles, a game that has broken up more marriages than the ancient sport of plate-throwing. Mixed doubles is altogether different. Sex determines almost every tactic. Suffice it here to repeat the definition by Art Hoppe, an American coach and cheerfully naked ape: 'The proper method of playing mixed doubles is to swipe the ball accidentally and straight at the woman opponent as hard and as accurately as possible. Male players

153

must not only retain equanimity on their side of the net, but create dissension on the other.'

Years and years ago – or rather, just as Hewitt and McMillan had the signwriters in, prior to getting their show on the road – I remember another marvellous double act, also from South Africa. Gordon Forbes was the straight man with the sliced backhand, Abe Segal the comic with the bow legs and the cudgel. They were more likely to lose semi-finals than to win championships, but their charms were much loved.

Forbes, whose memoir *A Handful of Summers* remains, for my money, one of all sport's best autobiographies, insists the cardinal rule for men's doubles is to watch the ball, never the opposing net player. Really good duos, he says, eventually develop a method of being aware of what opponents are doing while still watching the ball.

Of course, admits Forbes, anyone who had to play doubles with Segal would perforce have to spend more time watching his partner! Abe had an unconventional and forthright view of both life and net play which often verged on the methods used by bulls in their dealing with gates. His friend also had an intestinal plumbing system that was unique, not to say noisy and pungent, recalls Forbes.

On one of their first visits to the Foro Italico courts, Abe did as the Romans do and shovelled seeming miles of spaghetti down his throat the night before their first match. Lubricated with lashings of *Bolognese*.

Next morning Forbes went to change and found Segal already in the dressing-room and frantically busy with a packet of Eno's Fruit Salts.

'Jeez, Forbsey!' he said, 'that spaggie's hard to move!' Then he downed another foaming glass of salts and did up his plimsolls with a jerk.

Recalls Gordon: 'Throughout the match Abe retained an intense, anticipatory sort of look as though he wasn't quite sure of his immediate future. Once or twice as he passed on the way to the net after a big serve, I thought that I detected pressure leaks, and these suspicions were verified when we eventually led by two sets to love, 5–3 and my service to come. As I got ready to serve, Abie approached me and muttered through clenched teeth – 'Better hold his one, ol'buddy, or we may both never make it off court. You've heard of being swallowed by an avalanche – well, just bear that in mind.'

'With both of us, so to speak, under intense pressures, I held my serve. Abie shook hands very briefly and then set off for the locker-room at a sort of stiff-legged trot. No sooner had he disappeared inside, than I could swear that I felt a distant rumble: a distinct tremor that would, without doubt, have shown up on the Richter scale.'

One can't quite imagine such tales being told of those tight-lipped, millionaired, multinational corporations such as Taroczy and Gunthardt Ltd, or Jarryd and Simonsson Inc.

Miles Better

Everyone knows that Roger Bannister was the first man to run a four-minute mile. But how many, I wonder, remember Sydney Wooderson?

He immediately preceded Bannister in the nation's esteem. Indeed, but for the war, Wooderson would likely as not have been first inside four minutes. In 1937 at Motspur Park he set the record at 4 minutes 6.4 seconds. The unlikely, prim, stick-thin, South London solicitor was in his thirties when the war ended but still, swot's spectacles glinting and baggy shorts flapping, he continued to inspire the land for a year or two.

Indeed, Wooderson directly inspired Bannister. One of the last books I ever shoplifted, from Smith's in Stroud when I was still a short-trousered oik, was the young doctor's gushing student autobiography, *First Four Minutes*. In it he recalls the first time his father took him to an athletics meeting – at the White City in 1945, Wooderson top of the bill: 'I had never before watched anything more than school sports. Before we reached the stadium's gates through the throng, they closed them. There were already fifty thousand people inside. Someone pushed over a barrier, a police cordon broke, and before I recovered my breath I was inside the coveted ground . . . from that day Wooderson became my hero. He simply inspired me. I admired him as much for his attitude to running as for the feats he achieved. He was a methodical and unassuming athlete who was prepared to give up time and energy to encourage youngsters.'

Recently I tracked down Sydney Wooderson. He lives in quiet, serene retirement at Perranporth in Cornwall. He enjoys only gentle cliff walks these days. And sport on television. Yes, he was looking forward to the Olympics – 'though I suppose most of the events will be on at the wrong time of day for me'. And certainly he remembers May 6, 1954. He heard of it on the evening wireless news, and had been 'absolutely delighted' for the young medical student. He wasn't in the least bit surprised that Bannister was almost unconscious at the end of his epic effort – 'a lot of runners used to faint in those days'.

The boy Bannister recalls in his 1955 book (no ghostwriters for the middle classes in those days): 'I leapt at the tape like a man taking his last spring to save himself from the chasm that threatens to engulf him. My effort was over and I collapsed almost unconscious with an arm on either side of me. It was only then that the real pain overtook me. I felt like an exploded flashbulb with no will to live: I just went on existing in the most passive physical state without being quite unconscious. Blood surged from my muscles and seemed to fell me. It was as if all my limbs were caught in an ever-tightening vice. But I knew I had done it even before I heard the time . . . We had done it! We shared a place where no man had yet ventured – secure for all time, however fast men might run miles in the future, and in the wonderful joy my pain was forgotten.'

Follow that, Sebastian! And stop looking so damned relaxed on those laps of honour!

Bannister's time had been 3 minutes 59.4 seconds. It was broken only forty-six days later, at Turku in Finland, by the extrovert, bouncy Australian, John Landy, who preferred beach rugby till he was chain-ganged into 100 barefoot miles a week by the legendary Australian taskmaster, Percy Cerutty.

In August that year, Bannister and Landy met in the Commonwealth Games mile final at Vancouver. It was a sensational race. Landy led friskily through the three laps. Bannister loped, pale and worried, in his slipstream. On the final bend, Landy looked left as Bannister passed him on the right. It was an electric moment. Bannister recalls: 'As I flung myself past him, he glanced inwards over his left shoulder – a tiny act that held great significance. All round the bend he had been unable to hear me behind him, the noise of the crowd was so great. He must have hoped desperately that I had fallen back . . .'

Bannister won, both men breaking four minutes. The barrier was well and truly bust – though it is surprising that the world mile record has been broken by only nine men since. Before the remarkable Coe and Ovett started shuttling the thing backwards and forwards between them, the record was held by the cheery Huddersfield hustler, Ibbotson; Cerutty's new boy, the majestic Elliott, who found it difficult to be too devoted to his coach's *credo* that 'athletics itself is less important than achievement'; then there were the two All Blacks, Snell and Walker; the French dasher, Jazy; the solemn American, Ryun, and the twinkling Tanzanian, Bayi. . .

All of them watched on television by Sydney Wooderson at Perranporth.

TV Games

Why are television outside broadcast sports transmissions such easy and regular prey for the critics? Unfair game. It is a mystifying state of affairs, for TV sport – unrehearsed, unscripted, unscissored, *genuine* drama – could expect to be nursed and cuddled with affection and delight by such understanding and knowing sports enthusiasts as Clive James, Russell Davies and Julian Barnes. Even Herbert Kretzmer and Nancy Banks Smith are known to have very welcoming soft spots in there somewhere for any thespian-athlete. Yet, for the last decade or so, sport has been downed by one of them once a week at least and then, the following week, ridiculed to death by most of the others. Our Benny Green is (usually) the gleaming exception.

In passing, I often wish *really* bitchy critics like Osborne, Levin, Waugh, or Mortimer, loved sport (which they patently do not, though I may be wrong about John O), for at least none of them have ever been afraid to put on their flip side and holler their enthusiasms to the skies.

Perhaps, between the biff of their commas and the splat of their exclamation marks, it has been nothing but a question of jealousy. Clive James has already – and already tediously, for my money – shown that all he wanted was to be a TV starlet himself. He annually, cruelly, and agreed, wittily, attempted to turn Dan Maskell into a national buffoon; 'This Wimbledon, Maskell said "Ooh I say" a total of 1,358 times.

159

The trouble with Dan's style is that it's so infectious. Ooh I say, it's a really infectious style.'

Yet the nation remained adoring nieces and nephews of Dan – and now I'm pleased to report that they are delighted whenever they hear that that bully-boy evacuee, with the hair on his knuckles but not on his head, is said to squirm and rage whenever the same treatment is meted out to him.

For the others, might it be a question of 'You only hurt the one your le-rve . . .' like that old crooner used to croon? Because they don't waste half their valuable column space discussing the broad, and very debatable, issues arising from sport and broadcasting. They nit-pick. They wait in their lairs all day, twitching with anticipation while they should be watching 'The Money Programme' or even 'Omnibus'. They bug everything and everywhere – and then all at once, blessed relief! Hugh Johns, from some obscure football match in the Midlands, says, '. . . And the referee is looking at his whistle and looks all set to blow his watch!' – and that's it, kids, I've got my column for this week!

Don't get me wrong, I wouldn't mind in the least if they even mounted a concerted campaign for *less* sport on TV.

There is far too much. The Sunday before Christmas I was in urgent need of a siesta with a sepia-soppy afternoon film. Heaven! But my choice of four turned out to be the Cognac Courvoisier show-jumping stakes from Olympia (yawn); Abercynon v Maesteg rugger (yawn, yawn); Italian Dolomites men's downhill skiing (yawn, yawn, yawn); or a former nun talks to Malcolm Muggeridge on Channel Fourzzzzzzz. . . .

Those of you still awake, stand by for another *slugfest* for the critics which will be, for you and me, one of our too seldom opportunties to wallow again in the classics. Now yet another excuse for a party as BBC *'Sportsnight'* celebrates its 500th transmission and I think you can rest assured that they will really pull out and Sellotape together a pageant of, as the man said, *the big ones*.

There's bound to be little Don Thompson, like a Foreign Legion Chaplin, waddling up to the Colosseum in Rome in 1960, there'll be Arkle yoked up the slope with Mill House at Cheltenham, and there'll be Trueman's swaggering 300th, and Sharp's try, and Hancock's two years later when Peter West said, 'Oh, my God!'

Tokyo all over again – with Ken Matthews and his wife, and Lynn the Leap, and Golden, Golden Mary, and that stupendous surge by Ann Packer, at which, I swear, though it was twenty years ago, David Coleman has never since been hoarser.

They must give us Henry hitting Cassius ('My ancestors felt that wa-a-ay back in Africa!'), and Hurst's last goal on a golden day ('They think it's all over – *it is now!*' mellow-bellowed Wolstenholme), and the milk-float puller, Foinavon, tiptoeing through such Aintree carnage that had Michael O'Hehir squeezing his nose even more to call it ('a roight poileup an' all!'

We'll have Hemery and the Sherwoods, and Beamon, and Besson against our poor long gone, lovely Board. Then Mary P's smile again. Hear again Longhurst on Jacklin ('Well, I never . . .'), and Longhurst as Sanders bends to pick up that imaginary bit of fluff on the last at St Andrews – 'That's the sure sign he's bound to miss it' (growling pause) 'and there but for the Grace of God go all of us.'

There'll be Banks' save in a flash, and Carlos Alberto's last Pele-made goal, and Jack Bond's catch, and Botham's sixes, and Red Rum's fours, and Stokoe's hat, and the Ba-baas' try. And much more besides . . . Everything, from the Boat Race sinking ('this might even lead to a drowning problem') to last year's young Cram on the crown of the faraway bend. *'Has he gone too soon?'* Coleman's cry must have echoed round every other sitting-room in the land. He hadn't. Magnificent. What a show.

The critics are bound to pan it.

LONG DAYS...

Cricketing Heroes

A New Zealand cricket tour always represents the anniversary of the first Test I ever saw: the fourth Saturday of July, 1949, England versus the Kiwis on Cardus' 'greenest grass in all of England' at Old Trafford.

I was only tippling the Tizer then, as my freshly-minted, beanstalk-bright eyes gaped in awe at famous names made flesh: Compton and Washbrook and Hutton and Evans, Sutcliffe, Donnelly, Cowie and Burtt ... and the Kiwi stumper, Francis Mooney, who had the same Christian name as me.

It was also Brian Close's Test Match debut. I was aged eleven years and two hundred and ninety-one days; Closey was eighteen years and one hundred and forty-nine days and the youngest cricketer ever to play for England. He looked as scrawny-tall as a model girl and his National Service haircut was carefully quiffed and greased. The boy bowled upright-ordinary and took a mid-order wicket with a full toss. He batted at No. 9 with the need to get a move on. His neckerchiefed, yeoman captain, Freddie Brown, gave the orders at the wicket gate: 'Have a look at a couple, then give it a go'. First two balls the gangly lank played back to the bowler, Burtt – but firmly enough to make the slow left-armer wring his hand when he stopped them. Off the third ball, the kid let fly the game's most trenchant stroke, a cleanly hit, front foot pull-hoik off middle peg. High, higher and handsome it went to the arena's longest boundary under the railway line.

Rabone thrillingly caught it at deepest midwicket, leaning over the boundary boards.

A wicket from a full toss; a duck from the game's most exhilarating stroke. Desserts and rewards were already hard to reconcile for Close. It would always be so – though in my battered old scrapbook of heroes he has remained underlined in esteem and affection – not least because we shared a Test Match debut.

Another young man also made his first international appearance that golden day in Manchester, and though he was to become a far better Test Match all-rounder than even Close, I cannot remember a thing about John Reid's baptism. I have just looked up the bible: he was a month from his twenty-first birthday and he scored, apparently, a 'pugnacious half century'. Thereafter he played in the baggy black cap a world record fifty-eight consecutive Tests – thirty-four as captain, during which time he led New Zealand to their first three victories.

Reid really was a Renaissance cricketer: stonewaller, audacious hitter, fast out-swing, medium cutters, slow off-breaks, a daredevil fielder close-in or an exuberant swallow on the fringes of the square. At one time he held the New Zealand records simultaneously for making most Test runs, taking most wickets, holding most catches, scoring most centuries, and playing for and captaining the country most times, besides having made most first-class runs in all first-class matches. And I was witness to his first entrance – and cannot recall a thing!

When New Zealand fielded, I swigged my Tizer and kept my eyes on the wicketkeeper, Francis Mooney. It was the first time I sensed my Christian name might not be so cissy – or certainly not one to debar you from playing Test cricket – so I decided not, after all, to change my name to Vince next term. Mooney was also appealing, for I had been told his colleagues called him 'Starlight', because of his penchant for pm partygoing and cutting a rug in his dance-pumps. Francis, in a day, became an okay monicker.

Reid turned an arm for the first time in Test cricket, but the bowlers I remember were the spinner, Tom Burtt, a roly-poly; smiling Tony Galento, with a lick of his fingers and a couple of

...BUT I CANNOT RECALL A THING!

paces to the wicket; Jack Cowie, medium fast, who ran in – and in again – with the rumbling, threatening, chin-down, relentlessness of a rhino at practice; and Harry Cave, upright and military with an approach like he was hop scotching through a minefield before delivering, with relief and release, like a celebrating windmill.

New Zealand bowlers have always been hotstuff on quaint actions. Watch Bracewell, for instance, and take bets on whether his follow-through will turn into a schoolboy clown's joyous cartwheel; or Cairns, with his whopping great Cornish pasty hands and half off the wrong foot, like he was Mike Procter smashing at the net in tennis.

Nonetheless, till the arrival of the outstanding Richard Hadlee, it has always been the New Zealand batsmen that have logged in gold leaf their place in the game's long chronicle. Hadlee's father, Walter, captained that first side I saw in 1949. He was straight-backed, unsmiling, and bespectacled. He looked just like my Latin master. He had in his side two batsmen of superlative quality. They put on an unfussy three-figure stand at Old Trafford and even my untutored appreciation could tell that my England bowling heroes were toiling. Martin Donnelly and Bert Sutcliffe were both left-handed. Neil Harvey, the Australian demon, had emerged in the previous late summer, but still, for a year or two. Sutcliffe and Donnelly vied with each other to be the world's best left-hand bat.

Hitherto, only Bradman had scored more runs as a tourist to England than Sutcliffe's 2,627 runs in 1949. He was blond, with beautifully correct footwork and always seemed to be enjoying himself at the crease. Donnelly scored 2,287 runs that summer, including, by all accounts, a mesmerizing 206 against England at Lord's. He was short and sturdy, with all the strokes – a scientific hitter. He went up to Oxford after the war, thrilled the Parks for two seasons and also played one game – for England – at rugby union as a centre-threequarter. Then he was gone. He put his bat in the attic and became a director of Courtaulds in Australia.

Sutcliffe played on, to dominate with Reid most every New Zealand innings. In 1965, in the first Test Match at Edgbaston, he ducked into a flier from Fred Trueman and was helped from the field with blood coursing from his ear. He returned after treatment to score an heroic half-century – but was a passenger for the remainder of the tour; that, effectively, was that.

Brian Close, of course, continued for a decade longer than Sutcliffe. In Test cricket, he too was, to all intents, 'bounced' out – by the West Indian fast bowlers in a gruesome burst of savagery on a late summer evening in 1976. That was at Old Trafford, an unbelievable twenty-seven years after Close (and I) had made our first Test appearance. That night the missiles whirred angrily at the now bald head of the forty-five-year-old. Not once did he flinch. But the selectors thought enough was enough.

The Somerset opening batsman, Peter Roebuck, served his apprenticeship under Close, and has logged the one and only time that Close had been known to admit to pain. The rum old emperor was in hospital having his shoulder put back into joint, which can be excruciating. Yes, he finally admitted to the nurse, he was in agony. She was one of the ferocious types, and rebuked him: 'There's a mother upstairs having twins and she's not making a fuss.'

Retorted Closey: 'Well put them back in and see how she likes it!

120 Not Out

Take, if you will, the year 1864. It was a goodish twelve-month for a motley of reasons. One hundred and twenty years ago, for instance, Paraguay was playing Brazil – with guns; the British Empire was bothered by the Bhutanese in India, and becoming very angry with the Ashanti in Africa. *Our Mutual Friend* was brought out by Dickens; photographs by magnesium flash were taken for the first time in Manchester. They started building the London Embankment; Clifton Suspension Bridge was opened; and General Gordon captured Nanking. Oxford won the boat race by a rollicking twenty-seven seconds, and a white-faced chestnut, Blair Athol, won the Derby at Epsom in his first ever horse race.

There is, however, a vast congregation of men – from newly-minted schoolboys to softening, stubbled ancients – who insist that the very best thing that happened in 1864 was that *Wisden* hit the streets for the first time. (The year, by the way and appropriately, was also marked with a century at Brighton by a 15-year-old called William Grace, and a new, revolutionary, allowance at cricket for overarm bowling.)

John Wisden was a little fellow, and a guileful spin bowler. He was a founder of the line that bred men like Tich Freeman or Jack Young or George Emmett (who started with Gloucestershire as a leg spinner). Occasionally he turned to very fast off-breaks. In 1850 he took all ten, each clean bowled, for North versus South. He founded the United Touring XI. Once, when his team were sailing across the

169

Atlantic in mountainous seas, he remarked: 'What this soddin'
pitch needs is ten minutes with the heavy roller!'

When he retired, the jockey-sized tweaker set up a sports
shop and tobacconist in Leicester Square, London. His
business techniques were as snortingly competitive as his
nip-backing off-breaks. His rivals down the road, in
Piccadilly, were the brothers Lillywhite. They were
particularly hot stuff on snuff; they advertised far superior
foreign cigars and 'unrivalled shag'. They also started
bringing out an annual volume called *The Young Cricketers' Guide*.

John Wisden couldn't readily muscle in on the 'unrivalled'
shag imports. But for the Christmas trade of 1863 he
published John Wisden's *Cricketers' Almanack 1864*. Volume
One is now priceless. Before the laid-out scorecards of the
previous cricketing summer and the Laws of the Game, the
booklet begins with a long section of useless information so
beloved by the Victorians. The first line of the first *Wisden*
reads: 'January 1st – British Museum Closed.' Thereafter,
page upon page goes on to tell such as the dates generals were
born or when carpets were first made in Kidderminster. The
Almanack ends by nominating Tom Brett as 'The fastest and
straightest underhand bowler ever known'. Little John had
started a large institution.

There are new clichés now, to be sure, but it was long ago
that cricket writers gave up for Lent such descriptions as
'white willow whacked yon crimson rambler to the veriest
confines'. Yet still, each first week of May, they will
unashamedly welcome their 'primrose harbinger of the
spring'. The *Wisden* cover is gaudy yellow.

You pick it up and the winter is over. Just like that. Girding
the earth and the old Empire are tabulated the scores of every
first-class match of the twelve-month – and many second and
third class, come to that. Every run is notched, every leg-bye
logged, every ancient record is polished and preened, every
new one weighed and measured, departmentalized and
displayed. In over 120 years *Wisden* has had as many editors as
the *Daily Express* in the last twenty-five. There were ten before
the present editor, John Woodcock. Every edition, he queries
the last. Was last year up to scratch? Well, there are eleven
entries in *Errata*, dammit, including 'page 1209, Jack Redman

should read Jim Redman; he was christened James,' and 'page 964, in New Zealand's first innings there were 17 leg-byes (not 18) and 17 no balls (not 16).' Disgraceful! Watch it in future, will you, Wooders!

This year's edition of 1,330 pages is 32 up on last year. It is, says Woodcock, 'an increasing worry to know how best to make room for everything one would like to carry,' and 'close students will note a number of changes in this 120th edition, all of inclusion or adjustment rather than omission.' Not so, old cock! Shock! Horror! For the first time in (my) living memory the batting and bowling averages of my old school, Douai, have been ruthlessly excised. For a century or so we've sat there, snug, between Dean Close and Dentstone, and Dover College and Downside. Now I agree the figures have been pretty tawdry over the years – P12, W1 (usually versus the Monastery), L10, D1, or suchlike – but for Woodcock blithely to put a bomb under that mellow-pink, Berkshire-brick cluster of cricketing memories is sad in the extreme. We were jolly good at rugger, though.

It was, *Wisden* records, also a disappointing 1982 for the Lords & Commons XI. W4, L4, D3 and two 'abandoned owing to Falklands emergency debates'. The Almanack is an indipper in the Procter class. Every page a winner. Up to a year ago, in the Births and Deaths, we had 'Cowdrey, C. S. (Kent)' followed by 'Cowdrey, *Mr* M. C. (Kent)', because the great Colin played before 1963, the year 'amateurs' were wiped from the face of the earth. Now M. C. has lost his 'Mister'.

Even the Second XI notes turn up little treasures. The championship was won in 1982 by Worcestershire, thanks to the batting of 'the prolific Damien D'Oliveira'. Yes, son of Dolly! Runners-up were Lancs and Kent, 'challengingly' led, respectively, by Harry Pilling and Alan Ealham. So that's what happens? Old cricketers never die – they just go and lead the Seconds.

In any year, the Obituaries are the most poignant. Lately, there have been tributes to Sandham and Sealy and Slasher MacKay, to Muncer and Luckes and Lee, F. S. Also to 'Trumper, Victor (jun.), only son of legendary father; a fast out-swing bowler, with a few pretensions to batting.' Or what about 'Woodman, Reginald George, aged 84; he played two matches for Gloucestershire in 1925 as a batsman, but without success.' Or 'Franks, Brian Morton Foster, aged 71, a member of the Eton XI in 1929, he was a steady fast-medium bowler who had some life off the wicket.'

No more. No less. And so, from over to over, the great game goes on. *Wisden* logs you, intrigues you, and buries you. Who said corner-shop tobacconists lacked vision?

Game Keeping

The names of Alan Knott and Bob Taylor will be forever written in bold gold leaf in the legend of cricket.

Cardus defined the two types of stumper that history has allowed. Knott and Taylor fall respectively into his categories to perfection. Like the old man's Duckworth and Oldfield. Knott is the former – who might dismiss his man in a frenzy of mingled exultation, rage, and indignation. At a stumping chance his appeal says, at one and the same time. 'Out! How dare you lift your right toe? I'm here. Out! Hop it! Out, umpire, I'm telling you.'

Taylor is more the Oldfield of Cardus' time. He does his work by stealth, whipping off the bails quietly and turning his head to the square-leg umpire and formally asking 'How is that?' He seems to apologize to the batsman as though saying, 'Terribly sorry to have to stump you like this, sir – and behind your back! – but I have no alternative. Anyway, I'm doing it as nicely as I can, only the leg bail. Good afternoon; there's the pavilion on your right. Mind the step.'

The English game has been lucky with its wicketkeepers. Blackham and Huish and Hubble and Hunter, Butt and Board, Ames and Strudwick, Andrew and Evans . . .

The first appealer to appeal to me was a dead ringer for Sir Neville's Duckworth. Andy Wilson was a tiny tot. His gloves burrowed into his armpits, the top of his pads covered his tummy button. His shriek was so shrilly plaintive it would sometimes frighten even Gloucestershire's spinners, old Tom

Goddard and young Sam Cook. He will always be in *Wisden*, for one day in 1953, at Portsmouth, he took ten catches against Hampshire.

Andy fancied himself as a bat. Two years before the famous Wessex Wednesday, the West Indians came to Cheltenham. They were the first black men I ever saw, and they were gods. Weekes got a half-century and Walcott a whole one. Then Ramadhin and Valentine bowled. After all his years keeping to Goddard and Cook, Andy was so confident that he would read Ramadhin's wrong'un that he accepted bets on the fact before he was called to waddle to the wicket. Both innings he

shouldered arms to let the little long-sleeved mesmerist's first ball go by. Both times he was clean bowled.

Andy became the National Farmers' Union secretary somewhere down towards the Forest and sometimes still you can read his natty sports reports in the *Sunday Telegraph* West Country edition.

It wasn't long, mind you, till Andy became small beer, as us nippers began to rouse ourselves and realize that the world lay out there yonder. I suppose Godfrey Evans was just about the first national hero to every schoolboy of my generation. I can still in my mind's eye recall every exact detail of one of the first pictures I ever pasted into my scrapbook; 'Godders' at work as he whirled, in a blurr of musketeer's big red gloves and frightened little bails, towards the square-leg umpire in a raucous request for a stumping off Laker or Lock, or Tattersall or Wardle – or even the nippy Wright or Bedser or Bailey, for Godfrey was a standup comic, not a long-faced longstop.

Evans was one of Sir Neville's Duckworths – 'attacking from behind as directly and violently as the bowler is attacking from the front . . . a ravenous presence behind the wicket'. Evans was the monarch of a princely court of his time that included such as Brennan and Booth and Binks and Dawkes and, of course, the great Andrew.

Then there was an interlude for 'stoppers' who could bat. No man was better at that than Jim Parks, a good-natured cavalier with a smile a'twitch his lips. As a wicketkeeper he was a padded longstop, but he held most things that came his way and, when he batted, he would grip the handle at the top and swing with a marvellously graceful swish. Whenever I saw Parks keeping wicket, though, I would sigh for his teenage fielding at extra-cover. Once as a kid I saw him in the very freshness of his newly-minted youth give a thrilling exhibition of cover fielding against the drives of Graveney and Emmett. It was like Gordon Banks 'dominating the box', as the soccer writers say. So did young Jim Parks dominate the fringes of the square. Silken speed and swallow's swoops and throws that went like arrows. It was a tragedy that they talked him into wicketkeeping.

When new selectors, in their wisdom, turned to John

Murray, the traditional orders were re-established. He was sedate and calming and well turned out. He scarcely missed a thing. Remember his un-ending six-ball over ritual? From the bowler, or from a throw-in, he would softly nest the ball in his gloves, cuddling it into his armpit in a nursemaid's soft caress. Then he would set the ball back on its little necklace of catches to the bowler by throwing it, say, to gully, and this time his gloved right arm would follow through high, and he would hold the pose momentarily as if he was a stately waiter bringing on a drinks tray.

Then he would prepare to settle again: he would tap together three times the reinforced fingertips of his gloves before, in unison, they would be raised to readjust minutely the corners of the peak of his always-blue cap. On the way down fingertips would acknowledge each other again with just two friendly taps before, as he began to squat, the gloves would be gently opened, palms forward, like a spring flower, or to mix metaphors, like a proud jewel merchant displaying his wares on the unseen table before him. Then he would be down, knuckles kissing the grass. Ready! Play! Then the ritual again . . . and again.

Murray was an Oldfield – another gentlemanly Starkey of wicketkeepers. Then came Knott, in the line of Duckworth. Hostile and athletic and lithe, a worrier and a pessimist and a vibrant appealer. He will be much missed. So will the safe, trim Taylor, our Oldfield.

Howazee! indeed.

Good Ground Guide

August is a domestic month. The circus has left town. Petulant tennis players are stirring the dusts of other foreign fields, and the courts of Wimbledon lie serene and still.

No grunts assail the baselines, just the placid pick-pock of understrung rackets. All-England Club members may seem haughty, but deep down they are just genteel garden-partygoers who really do drink Robinson's Barley Water.

On the links at Royal Birkdale, no picknicking desert armies tramp the dunes as garish-trewed golfers blast, with sand and fury, or burn up the scrubland with their pars. In August, Rotarians and Round Tablers, with Lanky accents and grey gardening flannels, zig-zag up and down the fairways at pleasure and leisure. In August, the deadpan, tin-soldier playboys in their model racing cars have left the meadows round Silverstone to peaceful, munching Friesians – and so have the likable Lens in leathers, with Cheryls on the pillion, who invaded the shires at motor-cycling time.

August is for domestic, homely, cricket. August is for the county festivals. It is a month for a day in a deckchair at Eastbourne or Canterbury or Cheltenham, at warm and cuddly Weston-super-Mare or, later, at bracing, seagull-squealing Scarborough . . .

They are galas for boys who come to watch their gods, for the tired old men who nap. As Arlott remembered in his lovely poem:

> The members sat in their strong deckchairs
> And sometimes glanced at the play
> They smoked and talked of stocks and shares,
> And the bar stayed open all day.

Once, most cricketing counties booked their bands, pitched tents and hung bunting for the high-summer festival. There was Buxton and Blackpool, Southend, Harrogate, Dover and many others. Not many now take holidays to watch 'the cricket'.

I was brought up with Gloucestershire's August at Cheltenham. This year, come what may, I'll make it for a day at least. They used to have to close the gates when I was a kid. We'd have to get the first bus, over the top from Woolworth's in Stroud, to get a decent place in the queue that twined around the college railings. I saw the great, still remembered, match against Middlesex in 1947 – to all intents the very Championship decider – when, on a turning, drought-crisp pitch, the Londoners, Young and Sims, were too good for 'Glorse's' Goddard and Cook.

Goddard was my first idol. He took 2,979 wickets in his career. Only four men took more in the history of the game. Or ever will. Tom also kept a furniture shop in Gloucester. He was well over six feet tall. Dark, tanned like leather, and lined. He had huge hands and huge boots and a greedy stamina; he'd wheel and deal for wickets all day, a great floppy tent of a cream shirt billowing out behind him, his fizzing off-breaks spitting at the earth and the bat when they landed in front of the crease.

His appeal appealed. HOWAZEE! would reverberate round the fringe of hills above us from Cleeve to Birdlip. Even the Malverns shuddered. If an umpire was oblivious to a civil question, next time it would be a raucous and demanding HOWAZEEEE*THEN!* He used to buy his wickets. If he was hit for six, we'd never mind; he was still patiently spinning his deadly web for the foreign fly. 'Eh, Ta-am,' we'd shout when the autocratic captain, Basil Allen, helped set his field, 'whadabou' a bloke atop o' Leckhampton 'ill, then? C'mon

Ta-am, put a guy on the roof o' that there College Chapel, then!'

Goddard was born in 1900. He played till he was fifty. He died in 1966. As usual I'll think of him at Cheltenham week. HOWAZEE! And of all his other cronies ... doughty Jack Crapp, twinkling Georgie Emmett, titchy Wilson, farmer Neale, Barnett the fishmonger, Cook the plumber.

Cheltenham is a middlebrow festival. Canterbury remains the envied, upmarket job. Weston is down the scale – and, in a way, all the better for that. It's intimate, farmhand folksy, and smells, well if not of the sea exactly, at least of the Bristol Channel. The WI flower baskets at Weston are plumper and more colourful than at Canterbury or Chelt, but not quite so prissily arranged.

The Weston festival in August, wrote the game's very best light essayist, Robertson-Glasgow, over sixty years ago, 'was a thing of marquees where the right stuff could always be found, and deckchairs and wooden chairs under which the spade and bucket could be parked for an hour or two'. It's still pretty much the same, I fancy.

Richards and Botham are Somerset's mighty hitters of this era. They've always liked putting bat t'ball down there. In the 1930s it was Gimblett and Wellard. Harold was a thrillingly scientific smiter, Arthur a fast bowler who could occasionally slog sensationally. No-one was safe if he had his eye in. Once at Weston an ageing vicar was snoozing in a deckchair's summery curve when a steepling sixer from Wellard dropped out of the sky to form a crater less than six inches in front of the old boy's feet. It would have killed him. He opened one eye, looked down at the half-buried ball, smiled, then pulled his panama lower over his forehead, murmuring contentedly as he dozed off again, 'Good ol' Arthur.'

Note the scorecards. As Robertson-Glasgow said, 'Something odd always happens at the Weston Week.' Once, in the Royal Hotel, the captain of Surrey, P. G. H. Fender, complained to the manager that there wasn't enough room in his bedroom to swing a cat. The manager looked the Oval's city gent up and down. 'I didn't realize, sir,' he said, 'that you'd come down to Weston merely for the cat-swinging.'

Yet Canterbury fully deserves its reputation as the best of

the *fests*. The marquees are spicker, the white paint more span. Kent, in spite of the fidgety monkey, Knott, have always played a languid, gentlemen's game. Woolley, Cowdrey, Woolmer ... their traditions have been long tested and weathered. Canterbury has a Woolley Stand now, and an Ames Stand, but I doubt if the character, the *ambience*, of the Week has changed much since the St Lawrence Ground was opened in 1847. Beckett's cathedral, as ever, surveys the occasion from a distance; and in recent years, holding court on the ground itself, there has been an almost equally large and episcopal presence looking down from the heights. It is *le patron* – or as the writer, Peter Tinniswood, so gloriously named him: Mr E. W. 'Gloria' Swanson.

History will show Jim Swanton's fifty years as a cricket writer to have had an immense effect for goodness on the game, resoundingly so in such matters as the D'Oliveira Affair and the manners of man. A young Swanton saw one of cricket's best-remembered county hundreds at Canterbury nearly half a century ago – by 'Young Joe' Hardstaff, of Notts:

'The band of the Buffs would have been playing that August afternoon, and I sat under the old tree at the top of the ground with a bag of cherries watching this ever-elegant fellow dismissing the Kent bowling to all parts. In particular, with that generous backlift and both hands very high on the handle he drove with perfect timing into the pavilion geraniums at one end, and up to the tents at the other.'

That's *it*! Weston is toffee-apples, Cheltenham is plums – and Canterbury is *cherries!*

Action Replay

W. G. Grace did bat in old brown boots, and tauntingly raised his left toe to the approaching bowler. Bradman occasionally smiled as he plundered, and Compton regularly did. Miller didn't bother to tuck in his pad straps, and Woolley in fact looked nothing like Gower.

I don't know how many cigarettes Benson and Hedges sell at their 'Smoking can damage your health' Cup final at Lord's but certainly an extremely healthy spin-off for cricket lovers has emerged. The tobacco firm, in conjunction with the film agency, Visnews, have marketed for just under twenty pounds a ninety-minute videotape compilation which encapsulates the very history of batsmanship. The sumptuous parade of some two hundred batsmen, entitled 'Golden Greats' was devised, nurtured and written by David Frith, produced by David Puttnam, and is narrated by the inimitable John Arlott.

The earliest surviving 'action' picture of a cricket match is a static, upright change-of-ends shot during the match between Victoria and an England XI at Melbourne in 1862. From then on Frith's researches have unearthed some magnificent moving stuff. Mighty men in monochrome. Flannelled fools flickering to and fro for over a century.

We wondered what they looked like. Now we know, though sometimes, perforce, with only a few jerky glimmers. The shots of the Doctor – 'the mightiest of the mighty,' says Arlott – were taken in the nets, in front of a leisured straw-hatted group of watchers. Just half-dozen or so backward defensives or flicks off this toes. The left boot is raised, as the historians told us, and in the Champion's backlift there is a noticeable twiddly-diddly, a joyous little flourish that showed the old boy to be enjoying himself. The beard is in full bloom, to make him, as Arlott notes, 'as easily recognizable round the world as his Queen or his Prime Minister, Gladstone'.

Frith's flickering pageant spools on – Shrewsbury and Stoddart, the silk-shirted Ranji, the muscular Woods, the diminutive Abel, the lordly MacLaren – alas, no Jessop actually lighting any blue touch paper – he scored fifteen centuries in less than an hour – nor anything of Trumper except some larky poses at practice, a team-mate tossing up lobs. But there is striking newsreel of Trumper's funeral at Sydney's Waverley cemetery in 1915. Part of every Australian died with him, as the vast throng that turned out testified. Alongside the horse-drawn bier, you catch a glimpse of three pallbearers – Cotter and Noble, and, in a top hat, Charlie Macartney, the 'Governor General'. Said Charlie at many a breakfast, as he rubbed his hands with relish before tucking into his sausages, 'I pity any poor cove who's got to bowl against me today.' Macartney's famous century before lunch eleven years later was scored 'for Victor'.

At last we can actually see Hobbs and Sutcliffe go forth to bat for England – the Master calm, unruffled, shy; the Yorkshireman calm, unruffled, slick-haired, even dandyish; a partnership symbolizing not only English cricket of their times but the very definition of rocklike reliability. When Hobbs equalled Grace's record of 126 centuries at Taunton, the newsreel cameras were there. They had been followng him around for weeks. At the close of play on the Saturday evening he was 91 not out. On the Sunday they filmed him in his hotel at breakfast, lunch and tea. Monday morning, and with the cinema pianist in full triumphant tinkle, every run was logged till 99. The caption came up – 'Every ball bowled to him extracted a gasp from the multitude.' Then . . . nothing. Whether the cameraman had gone to the loo, was lighting up a Craven A, or was changing his roll of film is not known; but the historic shot was missed, and they had to recreate it two days later, with the cameraman on a ladder halfway down the pitch and the Master essaying a slow motion swipe to leg and scattering the hired-hand fieldsmen.

On and on . . . Woolley, the left-hander so often likened to Gower today, looked much taller and more gangly than the Leicestershire player, and much more of a fidget at the crease. Big Frank's bat was swathed in Elastoplast. We see Sandham's smile, a split-second snatch of Gunn's genius, Chapman in the unwithered bloom of his youth, Kippax's late cut, loaded with wrist, and Fender looking like an eager young Groucho – 'Golden long ago summers which left their warmth in the pavilion timbers of the land'.

Mead's shuffle at the crease, so beloved of old Hampshire men, was even more pronounced than the legend handed down. This most reliable, most painstaking left-hander of them all would delicately tap an angled bat in the blockhole, like a nervous niece at beach cricket, then chassis in on it just as the bowler was delivering. But he was extremely hard to dislodge. For fully thirty years in first-class cricket, he took guard, in Robertson-Glasgow's description, 'with the air of a guest who, having been offered a weekend by his host, obstinately decides to reside for six months'.

Mead's captain for a long time was Lord Tennyson. He was one of the few who could dismiss him. Sometimes Tennyson would arrive at Southampton or Bournemouth of a morning still in his dinner jacket. No problem, for Mead of course would be batting. His Lordship would have a bath drawn for him the better to exude last night's intake of champagne. As he was drying himself, and preparing to put on his pads, Tennyson would summon a Post Office messenger and dictate a wire. A quarter of an hour later, between overs, a telegram boy would run onto the field with an urgent message for the batsman. It would read: 'MEAD – GET OUT AT ONCE – TENNYSON.'

Then, of course, comes the relentless, athletic power of Hammond's 'proconsular presence', the mighty McCabe, Hutton and Headley and Hendren, Compton and Constantine, the three Ws – and all overshadowed by Bradman. The newsreel filming is getting better now and in close-up the little man is seen to put all-comers to the sword with ferocious pull after pull. When he comes in after 300 in a day at Headingley, the smarmy, anonymous, breathless commentator salutes him simply – 'Little man, you've had a busy day!'

184

In Bradman's last Test match innings, at The Oval in 1948 in 1948, he needed just four runs to give himself a Test batting average of 100. The England team cheered him when he reached the wicket. He was to face the impish Warwickshire leg spinner, Hollies.

A week or two before, when the Australians played at Edgbaston, Hollies' county captain, Dollery, had suggested the bowler should save his surprise googly for the Test Match. This he did, bowling only leg breaks and top spinners to the green-capped little demon. First ball at The Oval, Eric tossed up his leg break. Bradman blocked it. Next ball was the googly. Bradman was totally flummoxed, and bowled for a duck.

On the film, as soon as the wicket was broken, the whole ground was stunned. Even Hollies is in momentary disbelief. Only dear old Jack Crapp, at first slip, is seen to be clapping like mad. Just before he died three years ago, I asked Jack if the rumour was true that the reception for Bradman had so moved him that there were tears in his eyes and he was unable to see the ball Hollies bowled to him.

'That bugger Bradman,' said Jack, in awestruck recall, 'never had a tear in his eye in all his life!'

Boxed In

'Good morning, everyone. Morning, Trevor.'

'Mmm. Ahh. What? Umm. Poor ball, poorer shot, reasonable catch. Zzzz.'

'Morning, Sir Frederick.'

'Well, ah gi' oop, ah really do. Beggared if ah know what's bin goin' on aht there f'lasst three days. That Bob Willis. Ahm lost f'words, ah really am. E'en wi'a mickle an' a mookle, mahdog, William, could place 'is field better than you.'

'Morning, Blowers.'

'Mornin', Johnners, old thing. Frightfully good to be here, I must say. Oh, look at that pigeon flying near the roof of that spiffing red 39 bus . . . or is it a 54?'

'Morning, Alderman.'

'Mebbe f'some. Call that place an 'otel. Ah knew better at Nagpur on '82 tour.'

'Right, everyone, chocy cakers for the old double one-ers – elevenses. Golly, look. Two glistening pink cherries on the chocy. Reminds Blowers of Barbados, what.'

'Tee, hee. What-ho. Nudge-nudge. Say no more.'

'Make with the bubbly, Boil.'

'Leggo. Yaroo. I say, you fellows, let's not leave any for that swot, C M-J, what?'

(In the distance, a smattering of applause.)

'Coo, cripes. Some diminutive chappie must be out. Is it little Vishy? Or that tot, Gavaskar? Or one of those teeny-weenies from what's the new name for the place, Sri-Lon? All look alike to me. Tell us, beared wonder.'

186

Frindall reads the scorecard, after which Bailey says, 'Mmmm. Ahh. What? Umm. Poor ball, poorer shot, reasonable catch. Zzzz,' to general background effect of giggles being stifled with handkerchiefs and occasional spittled chocolatey pellets exploding on the microphone. At last, Johnners pulls himself together and expansively, even sexily, pops a glistening cherry into his mouth. He wipes the chocy from the toe of his spats, and says:

'Now let's go over to Wimbledon to see if it's stopped drizzling yet.'

The Test Match season gets under weigh in June and the boys from the Remove return to their little dorm above the pav. For the BBC radio's 'Test Match Special' ball-by-ball commentary team it is an important summer.

After more than than half a century of basking in the nation's esteem, they find themselves as an institution being sniped at. By their own kind, too.

For a year or two in *Radio Times*, and last summer in both *The Times* and *Guardian*, there had been letters of complaint from the cricket buffs about the suddenly juvenile standards of the broadcasting team. Then, in the October edition of *Wisden Cricket Monthly*, three whole pages were given over to the debate, with 'Distraught of Tunbridge Wells' mixing it something rotten with 'Leave Well Alone of Cheltenham'.

'I say to the whole sniggering, wine-bibbing, self-backslapping rump of a once dignified institution, "For God's sake go. You have been with us more than long enough",' wrote a Mr Heald, of Canterbury. His sort was answered at once by Mr Edsett, of Somerset: 'They should watch their bloody television instead' – or Mr Crisford, of Lewes: 'Send them a cake to cheer them up, and let's have the smoke from Fred's pipe coming out of their radios.' While the correspondence was balanced, the very fact of criticism might well have undermined the seemingly cheery composure of the chums. Bonhomie treads dangerous ground once it has to watch its step – especially in this case when, like most long-running serials, the cast in 'real life' are not half as matey or unbitchy as they seem to be once the compelling little red light goes on, and the signature tune starts up.

'Test Match Special' had bathed in the warm waters of

187

cultish appause for a long and, I would say, deserving time. Now here was their own 'in-house' magazine printing reams of abuse from cricket lovers, which included such wounding sideswipes as ' "It's a Knockout", on a bad day', or 'I listen with disgust, not having heard anything like it since the fourth form', while others fumed at hour upon hour of 'puerile comment,with Trueman's 'sour grapes', Mosey's 'boredom', Blofeld's 'ignorance', and Johnston's 'jokes, sweets, and concern for trivial side issues' while in the background the sacred sound of leather on wood 'is drowned by the clink of ice cubes and the fizz of tonic water'.

The bridge between national institution and national bore is thin and rickety. Ask David Frost, Anna Ford, the Editor of the *Sunday Times*, or even Ted Moult and his ruddy double-glazing outfit. In hindsight, 'Test Match Special' was going to be up against it from teatime on the final day of the Lord's centenary Test a couple of years ago when the players, even, paused to salute the broadcasters' eyrie high above the pavilion. It had just been announced that John Arlott was making his last broadcast commentary. And when he got up, turned his back on the cricket, mopped his brow with a great big hobo's red-and-white spotted handkerchief, and looked for a glass of wine after saying, 'And after Trevor Bailey it'll be Christopher Martin-Jenkins,' it really was era's end.

Arlott had begun his cricket broadcasts long before every ball was covered in every home Test Match. His first commentary, I think, described the Indians at Worcester in 1946. I first heard him some time in that golden summer of 1947. I was nine. Was it Jack Martin, of Kent, who was bowling? Or Harold Butler, of Notts? Anyway, I remember to this day Arlott's description of the lumbering walk-back, the turn, the twirl of sleeve and 'one-two-three-four-five-six-seven eight-nine-over-she goes . . . and he's bowled him'. You have to read it back with old Hampshire's mellow growl. I can give you, just about verbatim I reckon, Bradman's last knock at the Oval in 1948. Again, pretend you're gargling with the water of (appropriately) the Test. 'Bradman plays forward and it goes in the direction of the House of Commons . . . it doesn't go that far, of course, but just to Watkins at silly mid-off . . . Hollies again then . . . and he's bowled . . .

Bradman – bowled Hollies . . . nought . . . well, what can you say in such circumstances?'

When Arlott finally hung up his vowels after the centenary Test, the BBC's cricket producer, Peter Baxter, could have gone out to replace him just as, say, Selina replaced Anna. But as a broadcaster, Arlott was up on the plinth alongside Murrow and Cooke and grandfather Dimbleby. He was one-off, irreplaceable. So Baxter and his team soldiered on, but now without Arlott's overwhelming, melancholic, Wessex gravitas, the joky jollity was thrust downstage and, more crucial, without the eminence around, the carpers and critics dared at last to come out and play.

A very good broadcaster, surely, can only be himself. Nobody could remotely charge Brian Johnston with putting on an act. Though he is remarkably experienced and 'professional', he is one who alters his personality not one jot when the little red bulb lights up. Johnners talks just like that in real life. He has a permanent smile on his face. His autobiography was called, simply, *It's Been A Lot Of Fun*. He genuinely sees his role as anchor man at a transmission 'of four or five friends who would be at the Test Match anyway, just sitting around and chatting about it'. It just so happens that microphones are live in front of them. I don't know if Jonners actually likes chocy cake, but he certainly thinks it's a good enough jape if there at two glistening, pink cherries plonked on the top of it. He particularly enjoys anything ambiguous that he can get away with about 'balls', and relishes the day when someone is moved in the field to short-leg so he can stand there 'with his legs apart waiting for a tickle'.

Yaroo. Yippee.

Good morning, Johnners. Morning, Sir Frederick.

Morning, Blowers, old thing. Morning, everyone. Welcome back to one of the nicest sounds of summer. Make with the bubbly, Boil.

Down Under and Out

Forthcoming Australian cricket will be distinctly odd. No Test cricket side will ever again be Chappelled, Lilleed, and Marshed.

They left, as they arrived, together. They first played against Illingworth's England side of 1970–71. Thirteen years: an awful lot of Pommie-bashing. They didn't care at all for Pakistanis; they pitied little Indians and provincial New Zealanders; they snarled back, glare for glare, at West Indians; they might well have got on famously with South Africans had they been allowed to play them. But it was Englishmen they loathed.

Forgetting, for a moment, that the word 'cricket' still has, to some, connotations of chivalry, the three of them were quite superlative cricketers. Chappell, ever with an upright, cultured, haughty detachment, scored more Test Match runs than any other Australian – more than Bradman, more than Harvey or Ponsford or Trumper or Woodfull or Walters. Lillee, with the kestrel's cruel eye, the ominous drum-roll run-up and the classic side-on action, took more Test wickets by far than any of history's legendary bowlers – more, by a bulging sackful, than Gibbs or Sobers or Hall, or Trueman or Tate or Underwood. Marsh, squat as a mudlark scrum-half, with miner's forearms and gymnast's sprung heels, dismissed many more Test batsmen than even such revered and glittering glovemen as Knott or Evans, Murray or Struddy, Grout or Tallon or Taylor.

They worked together. When Lillee bowled, the other two took the tandem in turns. The legend 'c Marsh b Lillee' was inked into schoolboys' scorecards almost a hundred times in Test Matches – a staggering figure when you realize that history's next double act of bowler and padded henchman at the time was that of Botham and Taylor with 52 – followed, by the way, by such appealing duos as Grout/Davidson (44), and Oldfield/Grimmett (37), one more than Murray/Roberts for the West Indies, and Marsh's separate swagbag with Max Walker.

And if Marsh didn't pouch the nick from Lillee, more often than not Chappell, at slip, would. In his last Test Match a fortnight ago, Chappell beat Colin Cowdrey's record of 120 catches. Half of them were sponsored by Lillee's outswinger.

I saw them first on the Friday of the Lord's Test in 1972. It was 'Massie's Match', when Lillee's Perth clubmate bewildered the English with his massive, gently curling, frisbee swingers in the heavy, clouded, atmosphere. At the other end, the gangling Lillee had looked angry and menacing and fast. That afternoon, England hit back: Australia lost their openers for seven runs: Greg Chappell, as palely frail and straight-backed as a model girl, joined his shoulder-rolling, gum-chewing, combative captain and brother, Ian. They shored up the innings in a stand of 70-odd, the elder man lecturing the kid between every over. Epic stuff. When Ian went, cursing, the young man – who had not scored a boundary in those first three hours – plonked his left foot down the pitch and dismissed Snow, Price, Greig, Glifford and Illingworth to all points. He went to his century in the last over of the day – and next morning he was joined by the tubby Marsh, who peppered the pickets with six fours and two sixes in a merry half-hour. They had announced themselves to England.

It was later on that tour that, by chance, I shared a lift with the young Chappell. We sat together in the back of the chauffeured limousine. I started with time-of-day small-talk. I received not a single word in reply. When we arrived at his London hotel, the Waldorf, he was asleep. I gently woke him. He got out, and slammed the door without a word to me or the driver. Ever since, I have been in awe, or certainly wary, of his cold-fish disdain. Opponents, too, have been intimidated by his almost sneering silences. Tony Lewis said the other day that he did occasionally punctuate them, as he moved from end to end at slip, 'by letting the batsmen know an atrocity or two about their parentage'. But, for the most part, there seethed a contemplative *hauteur*.

Lillee and Marsh were always, at least, less sinister, more extrovert, about their Pommie-bashing. On the whole they were carefree confident that their deeds would outweigh their devilry. You dared ask for their autograph. Actually, one fancies that the two of them – at thirty-six, Marsh is eighteen months older – learned their first rudiments in aggro, not from the gangland boss, Ian Chappell, but from the captain who first picked them for the Western Australia State side, Tony Lock, the spiky, competitive emigré to Perth who used to bowl for Surrey and England with Jim Laker. Lock was not even afraid to pooh-pooh the chivalries of public school cricket within earshot of Peter May.

Lillee's longtime nickname was 'F.O.T.' Only dear friends dare call him so. It recalls the day, as a stringy colt in his first State season, that he was daydreaming in the deep, picking his nose at deep fine-leg. Bellowed the infuriated skipper, Lock, from short-leg – 'C'mon, wake up, Lill! Yer an Effin' Ol' Tart!'

Marsh, incidentally, answers to the name 'Bacchus' not because, as he once did, he beat the hitherto unbeatable

Douggie Walters in a marathon lager drinking contest – did I hear thirty-six cans of Swan on a flight from London? – but because there is a place in Australia called Bacchus Marsh. Actually, 'Romney' might have been slightly more original.

Together, F.O.T. and Bacchus have been involved in a few tawdry episodes. They each egg the other on, just as they do when they are concentrating only on the cricket. A few years ago, in Perth, Lillee went out to bat against England with one of his sponsor's experimental aluminium bats. When the England captain, Brearley, objected that it would ruin the ball, Lillee said he was quite prepared to leave the advertising gimmick at that – till Marsh, batting at the other end, insisted that he was quite within his rights to stay. The spoiled schoolboy's sit-down strike lasted fully ten minutes.

Neither of them admits who first came up with the idea to bet *against* their own team at Headingley a couple of years ago. The bookie says it was Lillee. In the last innings, Australia needed only 130 to win at a doddle. Marsh and Lillee secured odds of 500–1 that England would be victorious. England won. Lillee collected £5,000, Marsh £2,500. 'There was no question of us not trying to win the game for Australia,' insists Lillee – and with seventeen runs he was the third top scorer. But, for many cricket-lovers in Australia, the stench remains.

Even Marsh, however, thinks Lillee went too far the following winter when he spitefully kicked the Pakistan captain, Javed Miandad, at the wicket. One day, says Marsh, even Dennis will admit that was wrong. Lillee meanwhile sticks to his original story: 'It wasn't a kick; I just tapped his rump with my boot.'

The following season, against New Zealand, the crucial match reached a marvellously dramatic climax. There was one ball left and New Zealand needed just one sixer to win. Greg Chappell shamefully ordered his bowler to bowl an underarm daisy-cutter all along the ground. It was impossible to hit. The captain's long suspected meanness of spirit was at last fully revealed.

And yet, the great multitude of cricketers enjoy their game when – indeed, because – it is noble and generous and forgiving. Foes must be honoured. And the young Chappell, at the wicket, had a poise and grace and grandeur when he drove through mid-off that had been seldom matched in the long litany of lore. Alas, in a way, but his talent *did* outshine the poverty of his sportsmanship. And as Chappell stood there in the field, glowering grim at slip, next to him would be Marsh, gloved and padded, bouncy, bristling with belligerence and buried in his green cap . . . and, far away, the macho man, Lillee, would lick his right index finger as he turned on his mark; a preliminary stutter into his stride; then the momentum would gather, and so would the gale that billowed the back of his shirt, and so would the noise from the baying throng; now, as the gold chain whirled and glinted, the stride would lengthen, and the batsman would swallow, scared; the cocked grenade would be primed as it pumped away under Lillee's chin; the crowd's tattoo would reach crescendo as, in a feverish jingle-jangle of arms and elbows and legs, out would come the pin in a whirr and a stretch and a grunt . . .

Then Chappell, deadpan at slip, would unbend, Marsh, in the gloves, would return the ball with a smug, sadist's grin, and Lillee would set off back to his mark . . .

Three very missable men, who will very much be missed.

...LATE NIGHTS

Ring Pull

You can only rejoin the rest of the world by leaving Las Vegas. I don't go there for the gambling, but for the boxing. The boxing is only there for the gambling. The only time I have known an awful reality settle on the amazing place was the night, in 1980, that Muhammad Ali – slimmed down in a month from 256 to 217 pounds, his greying hair larded with Grecian 2000 – quit on his stool at the end of the tenth against Larry Holmes, and a tawdry *End* was writ to a once heroic *Legend*.

Nevada's desert range is a million miles from the plump green hillocks of Wales. There are no clocks in Las Vegas. They don't like to suggest to the gamblers that it might be time for bed. Fly in by night over the chocolatey desert with the last light of sunset making harsh cardboard cut-outs against the orange-gold sky. As the pilot dips a wing to prepare his approach from 20,000 feet, you catch a first glimpse down there of the neon nuthouse. It looks as if all the Vatican and Crown jewels have been strewn on a tiny strip of blue velvet. The illusion ends when, literally, you get down to earth.

In just two or three decades Las Vegas has offered the starkest possible historical contrast between the Olde American Dream and the New American Reality. Not long ago the place was infested by hopeful old prospectors who looked like Gabby Hayes, with a glint in their eye but not in their sieve; men who mined the mountains. Now the gold-diggers come to shoot crap, turn a card, or get fat on fruit machines. Or to have a fistfight.

It wasn't so long ago that Alistair Cooke came to Las Vegas for the first time for the old *Manchester Guardian* – 'to a dusty western town of a few thousand where I bedded down with a couple of cockroaches the size of mice; a town where water came from an artesian well, whose Chamber of Commerce was a one-storeyed stuccoed building, whose baseball park seated just 700, whose cottonwoods shaded still the relics of an old Mormon stockade.'

Once upon a time every ghetto kid's dream, as he chassied round the gym or worked the heavy ball or ploughed on with his roadwork at dawn, was to make a match for a fight in New York. The Polo Grounds! The Garden! Failing that, to be on a bill in Chicago would prove to grandchildren that an old fighter had once sniffed the blue cigar smoke of the bigtime. Now Las Vegas is the Mecca for professional boxing. The reason is simple: men who come to watch fights will stay and gamble. The big casinos – and I do mean *big*: imagine an underground room the size of the pitch at Wembley given over to serried rank upon rank of fruit machines, plonked next to a room the size of Lord's for roulette or blackjack – vie with each other to pay inflated prices for professional punch-ups. They are even happy to make a loss on the promotion, knowing they will recoup on the tables. The night Ali was humiliated by Holmes, Caesar's Palace flew in 2,500 of the world's highest rollers and gave them free rooms, free food and free tickets for the fight. It cost the Casino over half a million dollars. That week their gambling profits were up by six million dollars.

The local authority knows what's good for its town. Unlike the rest of the country, Nevada does not tax personal income. So fighters like to fight there. Before the casinos got in on the act, the Town Council itself staged big bouts at its Convention Center. In the 1960s, Fullmer, Tiger and Ortiz fought there. Ali, in his pomp, shone headlights in Patterson's eyes at Vegas. He buried Quarry there in his post-Vietnam comeback, and also had two exhibition dances against Bugner and Lyle, before his gruesome last waltz with Holmes.

Sometimes the very stuff of sport seeps through the seedy

business. I was there, some sweltering Septembers ago, when a spindly, menacing hitman from Detroit called Thomas Hearns lay in wait under the desert stars for a cocksure, whispy genius named Sugar Ray Leonard. It was an epic challenge; Hearns stalking, narrow-eyed and concentrating, his jackhammer right hand cocked and ready to explode; Leonard, an arrogant but half-wary smile forever creasing his choirboy's face, keeping out of trouble as if on a circus trick-cycle – backwards and forwards, and mostly sideways, left then right, ducking and bobbing, always that smile, always using the ropes like there might be a snakepit in the centre of the ring. Occasionally they came together for a snarling exchange of awesome, brief, brutality.

By the ninth, the metaphor was changing. Hearns' ammo was getting damp with sweat. The Fighter was fading and, as in the Classics, the Boxer had kept his powder dry. Leonard now circled the wagon with awful intent gleaming from his one good eye. Closer he dared, twanging in the odd arrow or three . . . By the fourteenth, the burning faggots started flying and Hearns was a goner. No Cavalry came to save him before the credits came up.

Sugar Ray left with the smile still playing about his lips. Hearns – neither cocky sugar nor spice, but the salt of the earth – is still treading the lonesome trail, though I doubt if he has another *real* fistfight inside him. He was carried out on his sword that night, and was in no fit state to go to the ball – but I dare say his bank manager was.

Under the moon that night, at the ring-side, Gerry Cooney sneered threats at the champion, Holmes. Six months later they were up there, stripped for action. This was dice for the heavy rollers. Black versus White – Mammon loves mono-chrome. Cooney, bejasus a great big broth of Blarney granite, was chipped and chiselled to nothing by the businesslike Negro. In the thirteenth, Holmes at last hit the white man with a real haymaker. It must have felt like a backheel by a Kinsale mule. 'Tank 'ee, sor, and goodnight. When he woke up next morning, Cooney said: 'I must really get myself some better sparring partners!' It doesn't seem that he has.

But always in Las Vegas I think of the end of Ali and the end of the twenty-year-old trail that had begun when the teenaged chocolate marionette had won the gold medal at the 1960 Rome Olympic Games. When he sat that 1980 night in his corner, cowled and cowering and *kaput*, it was the end of the pretence that professional boxing had any glamorous saving graces to it.

For two generations the wide world over, Ali had represented the daring and bravery, the skills and innocence and mischievousness of their youth. Now, quitting on his stool, he was a fallen, faded, jaded idol. He was, after all, fat and middle-aged like the rest of us.

Now boxing could be left to the unreal and awful idiocies of the Las Vegas gamblers.

Right on Cue

As the nights draw in with a vengeance, we have five months and the halls are alive to the sound of ivories – and I don't mean the grand and Winnie Attwell chopsticks variety.

The revival in popularity of snooker over the past decade has been in an exact proportion to the Technicolor revolution that has almost every sitting-room in the country cornered by a colour television set. Before then, snooker's clinking kaleidoscope of scarlets and pinks and greens and blues amounted to meaningless and fuzzy balls of monochrome wool. Now the commentators never need to repeat their lovely old whispered joke: '. . . And for those of you with black-and-white sets, the pink is behind the green.'

For potting black after black Steve Davis has been pocketing wad after wad of green. He was born only in 1959, yet he is far ahead of Henry Cooper, Edward Heath, or even Princess Michael of Kent, when it comes to an asking price to open jumble sales or supermarkets. He is a celebrity on late-night telly, breakfast telly, and children's telly. He has even hosted his own quiz show. Simply as a sportsman he will again, and unquestionably, be one of the most formidable figures in our winter's tale. As a snooker player the young man is a phenomenon.

I am not particularly well up in the misspent youths of others. I first came across his name some summers ago when I spent a rewarding day with Fred Davis, twinkling old cove of the cue who had seen it all in the half-century since his legendary elder brother, Joe, was first called 'The Emperor of Pot' by the *Derbyshire Evening Telegraph*. Is Hurrican Higgins the best, I asked? Or Ray Reardon? Or Eddie Charlton?

'No,' said Fred, with an extra gleam of certainty in his eye, 'I am convinced the best player in the world is a boy you have never even heard of. I've just done a little exhibition tour with him for Corals the bookmakers. Irrespective of his age, at times I knew I was playing with the finest player there has possibly ever been . . . and, funnily enough, his name is also Davis without the "e".' First Joe, then Fred, then Steve.

The coincidence of the surname is almost matched by the geographical one. Steve Davis was born in Plumstead, down by the wharves of London's sprawling eastern dockland and exactly next door to the old Woolwich Arsenal. Plumstead Road runs directly into Woolwich Church Street. And there, at the Royal Military Academy, the game of snooker was, indirectly, baptized.

Over a century ago, the Devonshire Regiment were keeping the Indian Empire in order. During the rainy season in the garrison Mess at Jubbulpore, afternoons before the first 'gin 'n' quin' of sundown were whiled away in the cavernous, be-fanned, and traditional old billiard room. Billiards was an ancient game, enjoying a fresh vogue now with the new rubber cushions and exactly rounded ivory balls.

Sometimes, for way of light relief from the skilful, and patient longueurs of billiards, the young officers played a game of their own invention – grabbing every ball they could lay their hands on and marking them with differing scoring numbers. In terms of colour they were, of course, only whites and reds. Attached to the garrison at that time, in 1875, was a young subaltern, later to become Colonel Sir Neville Chamberlain. Sixty-three years later he gave an interview to Compton Mackenzie, the novelist, and recalled the afternoon in that misty long-ago of Empire when the Devonshires' billiard room was visited by a new tyro tenderfoot just out from the Military Academy at Woolwich: 'In the course of the conversation he happened to remark that a first-year cadet at Woolwich was referred to as a "snooker", implying that this was the status of the lowest of the low. Like a public school fresher being called a newt. Indeed, the original term for a

cadet had been the French *neux*, which had been corrupted to "snooks" and then "snooker".'

Chamberlain went on to tell Mackenzie: 'The term was a new one to me . . . but when one of our party failed to hole a ball which was close to a corner pocket, I called out to him "Why, you're a regular snooker!" . . . and then to soothe the feelings of the culprit I added that we were all, so to speak, "snookers" at the game. Thus I suggested that it would be very appropriate to call the game "Snooker". The suggestion was adopted with enthusiasm and I understand the game has been so called ever since.'

The following year, Chamberlain left the Devonshires to join the Central India Horse. He took the game to the Mess and the clubs of Madras and then, in the summers, to the hill station at Ootacamund. It became the rage of the Ooty Club and the first official rules of Snooker were posted on the notice board of Ooty's billiard room alongside the Mess bills and garden announcements.

Snooker and billiards have a tender, loving researcher today in Clive Everton. In his classic history for Cassells, published in 1979, Everton takes the story further. One evening, in 1884, in Calcutta, Chamberlain was dining with the Marahajah of Cooch Behar. They were joined over the port by the very W. G. Grace of billiards, the black-bearded champion, John Roberts, a dynamic, massive Liverpudlian who was wandering the Empire selling his tables and giving exhibition matches. (When the Maharajah of Jaipur showed an interest, Roberts hired eight elephants to carry himself and seven tables from Delhi, clinched the deal and was also made 'Court Billiards Player for Life' at an annual salary of £500 as long as he came once a year.)

Anyway, that evening in Calcutta in 1884 ended with Chamberlain writing out Ooty's rules of Snooker for an intrigued and keen-eyed Roberts. Before you could say 'Joe Davis' he had wired them back to England. Roberts followed at once – and one of the first games he might have watched with the coloured balls was at the *Snooker* room in the Royal Military Academy at Woolwich . . . just down the road from St Nicholas' Hospital, Plumstead, where a tiny, sandy-haired bundle was born to Mrs Jean Catherine Davis some seventy-odd years later. And when the tot was two years old, on a whim, Jean paid two pounds at the Woolwich Woolworth's for a tiny Christmas present toy of a snooker table.

In a century, the very heart of the game had come back to Woolwich.

Short Circuit

Motor racing's Grand Prix season has a certain and clamorous finale at Kyalami in South Africa. As the BBC's supreme and strangulated tautologist, Murray Walker, once screeched through some other vrooming, fuming finish: 'The atmosphere is so tense you could cut it with a cricket stump!'

The garlands will go to the fastest. Kyalami is a high altitude, thin air track with the longest straight of all the championship courses. It is not a circuit for faint hearts, canny cornerers or those who fancy the delicate touch on the clutch. Kyalami is for pinning your ears back, putting your foot down and hanging on for dear life.

Ah! dear life. I am always sad when I think of Kyalami. Half-a-dozen years ago this week I had a lunch date with the young Welsh driver, Tom Pryce, who was universally presumed to be Britain's next world champion after James Hunt. It was the morning my new kitten got stuck up a tall tree. Tom arrived to pick me up in his Range Rover. I told him I had to wait for the Fire Brigade to arrive on one of their famous 'mercy dashes'. Daring, zestful, youthful Tom shinned up the perilous tree without a thought. I said I'd call the cat. 'Tom' and we went out for a long lunch and Tom told me his tales while his still-blushing and beautiful bride of two years, Nella, went shopping in Bayswater. At teatime I waved them off to Heathrow. They were going to South Africa, to the Grand Prix at Kyalami.

That was Monday. On Saturday Tom Pryce was dead. As

he turned his car into the straight on the third lap he was just a speck in the distance as an inexperienced race marshall decided it was safe to cross the track with a fire extinguisher. Tom was travelling at over 180mph. The marshall was about three-and-a-half strides from the kerb when Tom's car hit him. The fire extinguisher decapitated the driver.

So a friend became simply another tear-stained wail in the tragic litany of lives and loves lost in the name of his sport . . . Collins and Clark and Courage; Cevert and Spence and Siffert, Schlesser and Scarfiotti; Bendini, Birrel, Bonnier and Bruce McLaren; Riccardo Palletti and Giles Villeneuve; Rodriguez, Revson and Rindt . . . and they are just the names I can roll-call offhand.

At lunch a week before, Tom Pryce had resisted philosophizing about death. 'I don't say I don't fear it. But would I feel it? I am only really frightened of it for what it would do to those I leave behind.' He left behind Nella, a former teacher who was going to open a riding school in the heart of the south-east's Thelwell country, and a grieving father, who was a village policeman in rural North Wales and would always be left wondering if his son's life might have been spared had they not gone together to watch Fangio v Moss at Aintree when Tom was still in short trousers. They had perched perilously on an advertising scaffold to cheer Moss home.

Since that day, and the resulting school-boy passion for speed – even on his uncle's tractors – Tom's anxious mum always 'knew deep down' that it might end as it did. If ever they went to watch him drive she would creep in to the team caravan and pretend to listen to the radio commentary. 'Nothing could be as bad as actually watching.'

The 1984 season has been the 'safest' for many years. Perhaps modern motor racers at last see their pastime as lethal big business to be taken carefully and not as a sort of animated sepia print from the 1950s when the Marquis de Portago or a young Stirling Moss would win races at Silverstone in a short-sleeved cricket shirt, a Rockfist Rogan leather helmet and a pair of goggles from Timothy Whites. Those dashers sat upright, occasionally adjusting their wing mirrors as they pottered along; they would wave to their favourite hyphenated-hooray blonde groupie as they passed the pits, and you could recognize them by the set of their face, not only by the adverts their locked-in combustible tube was displaying. Timothy Whites do not stock underpants that allow you fifteen seconds' grace to unstrap yourself from an inferno.

Moss almost bridged the gap between the carefree and the careworn. In 1963 he was unconscious for twenty-five days after crashing at Goodwood. It was his last big race. He remembers waking up. 'There were purple flowers all around the hospital room when I finally opened my eyes and I thought golly! I'm in heaven.'

Jim Clark, who some still consider the best driver of them all, did bridge the gap between the olden days and the pill-popping, narrow-eyed new. I once met him at a party. He was a smiler, seemingly at total ease. Nobody worried for him, he was so smooth and calculating and capable. Six months later he wrapped his car round a tree at 160mph on a rainy day at Hockenheim, and only then did I remember that the suave man at that party – the coolest, calmest champion of them all – bit his fingernails almost down to the knuckles.

Jackie Stewart's first Grand Prix buddy was Clark. They were both Scots and were flatmates. His next great friend was Jochen Rindt. He died too. 'I keep seeing Jochen lying in the ambulance and his left foot dangling down, and Nina his wife screaming that we were all mad when we wouldn't let her go to him and then her sitting all alone with her eyes totally empty.' Stewart retired in 1973 after his third World Championship victory. Since then he has campaigned with a fervent zeal: no-one has been more heroic than Stewart in attempting to make safer his blood-soaked, smoke-plumed sport. He continues to be vilified by a handful of gruesome gawpers who hang onto the game's shirt-tails, for demanding more safeguards for drivers. On the whole he has fought a triumphant, winning battle. I visited him at his deservedly opulent home in Geneva – the jagged, snowy peaks craning above and the serene lake glistening 2,000 feet below. He said he knew I would ask, so he and his childhood-sweetheart-wife, Helen, had lain in bed that morning and counted all those friends or acquaintances in motor racing who were now *late* friends or acquaintances. 'We gave up counting when we reached sixty-three.'

On other mornings, Jackie tells, he sometimes wakes up chuckling. 'It comes on like a giggle, irrepressible, like champagne bubbles at the back of your nose – and I lie there in my big wide bed, perhaps here, or in the Connaught or the Plaza or the Georges Cinq and I laugh and laugh.' Why? 'Simply because I got away with it!' He escaped with the fortune and the fame, with the love and the loot. And now he wants his successors to be able to do the same.

After poor Rindt, Stewart's great friend was the dashing French boy, François Cevert. He was also his team-mate and protégé. François died at Watkins Glen, during the American Grand Prix in 1973. The first thing you notice as you walk into the hallway of Stewart's home is a tender portrait of young Cevert. Two days before he died, I hoarded this quote from the young, charming, seemingly indestructible Frenchman:

'There are two options in this game of ours, neither of them very appealing. You can quit racing and save your life, or you can quit racing and lose what life is all about. Anyway, there is no time to think of accident and tragedy – the circus goes on and circuses have no room for tears.'

Sport can only be about winning and losing, never about living or dying. If the drivers come unscathed through their historic dice in South Africa they will have made the Grand Prix season the safest in at least three decades. More than any other, Jackie Stewart will deserve the credit for it. For his safety campaign alone he must be in line for a knighthood.

Perhaps, at last, the old saying no longer applies – that the only way to win at Grand Prix racing is to quit when young. Then again, how young is young? At Kyalami, I will be thinking of young Tom Pryce.

Speakers' Corner

Spring is the season of club suppers. For sportsmen, an end of season approaches, but so does a beginning. The Catering Committee comes into its own at last.

March is dinners and dances and drunken dramatics; wine, cheese, and buffets; stags at bray. And speeches: 'Unaccustomed as I am . . .' with old jokes, in-jokes, dirty jokes, and tin-plate plaques and pots presented 'with our esteem to Mrs Jenks, who must be the longest serving tea lady in our Shire.'

For a month or so, expectant cricketers will not only be oiling their bats, but pressing their Sunday suits for Saturday's supper. Golfers too – except for those obsessive, hooked, non-hookers who sou' wester round to Winter Rules – will not only be eyeing up catalogue ads for those natty, Rupert Bear, bum-clinging bags of summer, but also trying to catch the captain's eye to see if they have at last been chosen to put up the 'famous' guest speaker for the night. Or even just pick him up from the station.

This is the time of year when a park footballer's most deadly enemy is suddenly his best friend and fellow inside-forward. For twin strikers become estranged, and pass not a pass, when vying for the supper's presentation of the 'Sunday Seconds' Leading Goalscorer of the Year' statuette. It is invariably topped with a crude, uncrafted, brassy mould of Tommy Lawton instepping a whizzbang, and in my day they used to be bought by the club treasurer from the Fancy Goods counter of Timothy, White's and Taylor. (The job then was to find a backstreet engraver; when you do, always make him an hon. life member.)

Rugby dinners are not, on the whole good news for outsiders. The macho bonhomie of the rugger buggers is a difficult act to understand, let alone break in on. True, some of my best friends play the game, and I'm sure they always start their annual end-of-season suppers with good intentions. But it has never been the same since that beefy, balding, bullock of an England prop-forward, Colin Smart, went public in Paris a couple of winters ago and was carried out of the stately post-match banquet after downing, by way of variety to the tang of some outstanding vintage wines, a bottle of after-shave lotion. The Freemason's code was broken, and now at rugby dinners I quite expect to see *Château Spice Ancien, Xmas '83* quoted on the bill of fare. Certainly they act as though it is.

Perhaps Colin was driven to it by the speeches. It seems hardly believable, but French after-dinner orators are more full of wind and pomp than those of Britain. That's why cricket suppers are probably the best: cricketers are seeped in the legend of their game. Agreed, at cricket do's the speeches are just as long, the presentations just as endearingly

domestic, the dress sense of I-say-have-you-met-the-good-lady-wife just as garishly wrong; the club Romeo, as ever, reeks of talc and has nail-clippered his moustache to an even racier angle, but even in his white tux, is still seen to be just all talk with every blonde bux. And 'Strangers in the Night' always precedes 'The Last Waltz', 'Auld Acquaintance', and Now Everyone Let's Have Three Cheers for the Retiring Captain.

Cricketers, above all games-players, set store by antiquity; possibly because no-one knows just how old cricket is. That most charming and original of all cricket writers, R. C. Robertson-Glasgow, once defined the sports-supper speech: 'If some one gets up and says that he saw the Blackburn Rovers beat the something-or-others in 1891, he might just as well have stayed in his seat; but a man who saw W. G. Grace cracking them around at Bristol in that year has news-value and an audience. He may be a howling bore, but he saw the Doctor in action.'

And so the speeches at cricket suppers are fond of secretaries who have been at the job for over fifty years, and of umpires who have stood for the village, man and boy. Scorers under sixty are not to be trusted.

Grace himself never bothered. He had one set speech when called upon as the port went round. On an early MCC tour to Canada and America, his first speech was at Montreal. 'Gentlemen,' he said, 'I beg to thank you for the honour you have done me. I have never seen better bowling than I have today, and I hope to see as good wherever I go.' He never varied it, except to substitute the word 'bowling'. At Ottawa it was 'a better pitch', at Toronto 'batsmanship', at Hamilton 'fellows', at Niagara 'prettier ladies', and in New York it was 'tasted better oysters'. Grace didn't go much on the graces; in his last years he admitted, 'I never had pretensions to oratory, I would any day have soon made a duck as a speech.'

One of cricket's very best after-dinner speakers since the war has been J. J. Warr, the former Middlesex long-run trundler. (Since the Warr, by the way, Henry Blofeld and Christopher Martin-Jenkins, an outstanding mimic, have been top of every supper secretary's list.) Perhaps Warr's two-Test batting average of Inns. 4, NO. 0, HS. 4, Av. 1.00, and bowling of Overs 94, Runs 281, Wkts. 1, Av. 281.00, made him thereafter concentrate on cricket's *après ski,* and he certainly became the game's most fluent, witty, and bluffest buffet buff.

Once he told of attending the Mumbles Cricket Club dinner at which the senior speaker who followed him was a hugely distinguished Welsh figure, then working in London. 'To give you an idea of the travel involved,' says Warr, 'Swansea is regarded as a suburb of Mumbles and the round trip from London is some 430 miles.'

On arrival on the appointed Friday evening, a local solicitor first did the honours with some typical Welsh hospitality in his home – ninety-nine parts gin to one part tonic. The meal was held at the local hotel. Further refreshment circulated freely. The distinguished guest partook, and was seated with his back to a radiator, 'to make the various drinks inside him ferment and curdle nicely inside him'.

At 10 pm the chairman spooned the table proudly and called upon the great man to put the final gloss on the evening with the speech proposed 'To Cricket'. He rose to his feet, his lips twitched, but no sound emerged.

Warr gloriously recalls the moment: 'It was at that point that he offered the greatest compliment that has ever been paid to a single cricketer. For through the mists of alcohol one single vision must have emerged, perhaps a cover drive perfectly executed. 'Wally Hammond was a jolly good player,' came the words erratically delivered but nonetheless sincere. And then came the slow but definite collapse of the speaker.' Whichever way you look at it, it works out at over sixty miles a word.

There is a lot of it about during March and April . . . slurring, unsteady, *Laydeez 'n' gennlemen, please charge your glasses to our great game of* . . .

Not forgetting the tea ladies, of course. God Bless 'em!

Name of the Game

Some time ago a boxer from South Carolina called Danny Sutton came to London to fight. Sutton was an unlikely American, for in the pre-fight bally-hoo and how d'y'do he uttered scarcely a word. His demeanour in the ring was just as deadpan – expressionless, he took a few and gave a few. He left next day with a reasonable cheque, a badly cut eye, and not so much as a goodbye. Yet emblazoned across the back of his dressing-gown – his 'fightin' robe' as they like to call it – had been the single word 'SMILEY'.

Sportsmen's nicknames are themselves pretty drear and deadpan things. Sutton's Smiley syndrome was obviously from the same department of irony that has the introverted cricketer, Tavare, called 'Rowdy' and the late Australian blocker, MacKay, called 'Slasher'.

There are two distinct types of nickname: those invented by dressing-room wise-guys, as in 'Chilly' Old (C. Old, geddit?) or Graham 'Picca' Dilley; and those invented by old-style newspaper sub-editors with an awful lot of headline space to fill, as in 'The Lion of Vienna' or 'The Emperor of Pot'. But no inside-forward colleague in those old Bolton Wanderers soccer teams would have actually shouted to Nat Lofthouse, 'Outside you, oh great Lion of Vienna!' or challenged Joe Davis at the Locarno, 'Care for half-a-crown's worth of bulb-time, oh Emperor of Pot?'

Boxing has had most of such sub's soubriquets. I suppose 'The Brown Bomber' for Joe Louis remains pretty trippingly in the common man's usage; but not Jack Dempsey's 'Manassa Mauler', and certainly not Jimmy Wilde's 'Ghost with the Hammer in his Hand'. That really was late-night Fleet Street desperation. Or drunkenness. That splendid character and champion of the 1930s, Max Baer, who hailed from a hog ranch at Livermore, some fifty miles from San Francisco, once listed all his old billings – successively he was the Livermore Larruper, the Livermore Butcher Boy, Madcap Maxie, the Larruping Lothario of Pugilism, the Pugilistic Poseur, the Clown of Clout, the Playboy of Pugilism, and the Fistic Harlequin.

We now call Bugner, Joe, and Bruno, Frank. How tedious. Half a century ago the British heavyweight champion was a Londoner, Phil Scott, who once won nine successive fights on a disqualification. He was known to one and all as either 'Fainting Phil' or 'The Swooning Swan of Soho'. Not long after Phil came another heavyweight, Jack Doyle, who was known as the 'Irish Thrush' for his habit of singing in his corner before a bout. He was an awful fighter. Once, while he was singing 'Mother Machree', his second at the ringside whispered to nobody in particular, 'Ah, if only he could fight her instead of sing her.'

Tennis, though not particularly original, is probably the most succinct these days, though even they are inclined to go occasionally for such unlikely descriptions of net styles as 'The Boy Octopus' for Frank Froehling or 'The Leaning Tower of Pasadena' for good soldier Stan Smith. But 'Muscles' for Rosewall, or 'Rocket' for Laver has gone into the language. The circuit will still lovingly recall the good old days of 'Hippy' (Ray Moore) or 'Nails', the languid Aussie carpenter, Carmichael. You just have to say 'the Brat' and they'll know you mean 'the Kid' (McEnroe). Even in his thirties, 'Jimbo' remains perfectly good for the combative Connors, as does 'Smartina' for the millionairess former Czech chick. And 'Nasty' could not have been more nicely appropriate.

The dreariness of this last winter's Rugby Union championship seems reflected in the lack of originality in the names. I remember in the 1960s when the England front row consisted of 'Piggy' Powell, 'Batman' Fairbrother, and 'Yeti' Wightman. This season the terrible trio were called Gary,

Colin and, the one concession, 'Brace', as in 'Wheelbrace' for the hooker, Wheeler. Yawn, yawn. In olden days, 'Pinetree' Meads said it all. 'Broon of Troon' rang nicely, as did 'Baz', for Basil Brush, as in the chirpy, bearded John Taylor.

His fellow players really did call Barry John 'The King'. His team mate, John Lloyd, was known by all as 'Greedy'. Before a match, the excitable coach, Clive Rowlands, was hyping up the Welsh team:

'And what are you going to do, John? What are you going to do if your English marker gets anywhere near you. What are you going to do?'

'I'll . . .' stuttered the hyped-up Lloyd, searching for the right word, 'I'll . . . I'll EAT 'im!' Mr Greedy was baptized.

I suppose 'Merve the Swerve' was okay if Davies had done much of it; but usually he was burrowing around on the ground. 'Japes' for the original J. P. R. Williams was fair enough and obvious. On the other hand, I suppose it depends on whom he was practising his japes. In the 1920s, England played a barnstorming military forward called Lt.-Col. Charles Faithfull, who was known (not, alas, as Marianne) to his own side as the amiable 'Chubby', but to his opponents as 'Mad Bull'. In the bar afterwards he would answer to both with not the flicker of an eyelid.

In motor racing, 'Hunt the Shunt' was pretty spot-on in Master James's L-plate days, but you'd think cricket, being the most reflective of games, would be the most original. It isn't. The opening bowler, Arnold, now of Sussex, is called 'Horse' because his initials are G. G. The wicket-keeper, Taylor, is called 'Chat', because he takes his ambassadorial mingling very seriously at tour cocktail parties. The nippy Randall is 'Arkle'. Gooch is 'Zap' because of his *bandito* moustache. The blond Leicestershire pin-up is 'Lulu'. You do occasionally hear Botham called 'Guy' as in Gorilla, but usually it is just 'Both' as in broth not in oath. Willis is 'Goose', and he sure runs up like one. The former captain is simply 'Brears', though in Australia they sneeringly called him 'Ayatollah'.

Brearley's opposite number over there, Ian Chappell, found himself with the most appropriate monicker, for he often gave the impression of running his team like a gang-land boss. The

216

capital-letters scoreboard at Melbourne would have him simply as 'CHAPPELLI'. His wicket keeper, Rod Marsh, is called 'Bacchus', not because of his drinking capacity but because, boringly, there is a place over there called Bacchus Marsh. (Come to think of it, why didn't we call our one-time Cockney soccer hero, 'Romney'?)

Soccer is baptismally dismal. It's all Shilts and Wilks and Robbo, Ballie, Nealo and Thommo. One of Rodney's old Fulham colleagues was a cheery but hesitant goalie with pat-a-cake palms called Peter Mellor. His butterfingers lost the 1975 Cup Final. Bobby 'Mooro' Moore christened him 'Daffodil' – because he only comes out once a year!

The Yanks have the right idea, even at soccer. A few years ago, after the 1978 World Cup, the American soccer team, Chicago Sting, signed a very likely Polish midfielder called Rikki Duda. So impressive did he look in his very first game that by the time they left the dressing-room for the second-half, all his team mates knew him simply as 'Zippity'.

Up for the Cup

The long held Scoutmasters' theory that sport and booze do not mix has taken a terrible hammering of late. If Mrs Whitehouse's mob were not so obsexed they could do the temperance societies quite a favour by starting to log the consumption on television of vodkas-and-lemonade by the snooker players, and of mild-and-bitter – and the other half, too – by the darts boys. When that truly epic voice crescendoes out 'One-hundred-and-*eighty!*' to raucous applause, I always get the feeling that he's announcing the pints consumed. Double-pops, not double-tops.

After the splendid, toothless, young Jocky Wilson, of Kirkaldy, had won the 1982 world darts title, he held a victory press conference. Suddenly, the smiler looked pained and put-upon, a Fifeshire McEnroe: 'Gentlemen,' he said, 'you have had a good go at my drinking habits, I would ask you to bear this in mind. Most darts players put away a few lagers or vodka and Cokes *before* a game. We do not keep up the pace or quantity during a game.' His italics. Anyway, it did not stop the Edinburgh song-smith, Bill Hill, celebrating their dentured hero's triumph on the local radio next morning:

'He's sixteen stane of fat and pain/When he steps up to the oche,/When he throws the spears you can hear the cheers/For Fife's wee hero Jocky./With an ample rear 'cos he thrives on beer,/Especially pints o' heavy,/He'll drink no Pimms or large pink gins/Or such exotic bevy.'

The most gorgeously dramatic case of what you might call

drink-and-driving I have witnessed was on the Indian plains at Indore in mid-January, 1982. I was travelling with the England cricket team. India is not what you'd call a drinking man's trip. For some reason we struck lucky at Indore. They were a super bunch of fellows to have a hooley with. There was a good one that night at the bar. Last two to bed – the barman was already asleep on the floor of his dispensary – were that astonishing champion of champions, Ian Botham, and myself. I had a fearful head next morning and only just groped my way to the team bus in time.

Ian was already on the bus. It had been quite a night, we agreed. I also remembered he had promised 'a bit of humpety' in the morning. England batted. Ian had a lie-down in the pavilion – though not for long. Tavare went at once, then Fletcher, his captain, and Cook, Ian's good friend who was playing for his Test place, were both given out on highly questionable decisions.

Somerset's celebrant of swipe strode in none too pleased. He took some time adjusting the sightscreens and his bleary eyes to the glare. He played himself in with untypically heavy menace. He blocked his first eleven balls. In the next forty-four, he hit sixteen fours, seven sixes, three twos and ten singles. When Ian had arrived at the wicket, his partner, Gatting, had not yet scored. When Ian was out – for a power-crazed 122 – Gatting had reached three. Ian had an early siesta on a dressing-room floor . . . then went and played a long game of badminton!

We had the other half that night. Well, already Botham at Indore had the same ring in the legend as Jessop at Hastings and Harrogate, Fender at Northampton, or Gimblett at Frome. (Incidentally, the night before Jessop's electrifying 102 at the Oval he had been up all night playing cards in King's Cross.)

We must continue to relish and savour the singular glories of Ian Botham while he remains among us. Some of the niggling criticism he is subject to appalls me. He is heir to that direct line from Jessop, through Compton. . . .

Ah, Denis. There was another folk hero who would stop for a quickie and the time of day with any man in the nation. That's why they loved him so. Still do. You cannot walk down a city street or a country lane with Denis today and the instant recognition doesn't bring a cheery smile to long faces or perkier birdsong from the hedgerows. We knew how to treat our Gods in his day. Like Botham, Denis also loved football. But he played in the days when the seasons allowed you to split your year at the two games.

Compton's last professional soccer match was the Cup Final of 1950. His gammy knee had had it. Against Liverpool, Arsenal were leading by 1–0 at half-time, but Denis, the left-winger for the Gunners, knew he had been playing like a drain. Had substitutes been allowed then, he admits, he would have been 'benched' already. In the concrete dungeon that serves as changing-rooms under the Wembley tunnel, Dennis was greeted at the interval by his manager, Tom Whitaker. 'Look, son,' he said, 'you have only got another 45 minutes to go in your whole football career. Pull yourself together and go and play a blinder for yourself and us.'

Says Denis: 'But I knew I couldn't. I slumped on the wall. I was absolutely snookered.' Wee Alex James, Arsenal's former pantalooned inside-forward wizard, was now the team's trainer and odd job man. He signalled Denis into a private shower cubicle. 'Here, laddie,' said Alex, 'get this down ye.' It was a large brandy – and then some more.

Compton bridled. 'I can't drink that! Not at half-time in a Cup Final!'

Insisted Alex: 'Get it down ye!'

Denis took one large slug. Then two. He wiped his mouth with the back of his hand before rejoining his team mates.

He went out and played his blinder, helping run Liverpool ragged, and contributing to the second goal for Lewis. 'The funny thing was,' recalls Denis thirty-three years later, 'that I never ever was a brandy man. And it's still one drink I never have.'

Then he burrows into the recesses. 'In fact I think the only time I remember having a large brandy before Alex's in that Cup Final, was two years earlier, in the summer of 1948.'

That year Bradman's invincible Australians cut a swathe through the land. In the third Test Match at Old Trafford, the ferociously glorious and hostile opening attack of Lindwall and Miller yet again had England on the rack. The first two wickets went for next to nothing – it was poor little George Emmett's solitary Test Match – and after he had made but three runs, Compton's temple was cut when he lost sight of a Lindwall thunderbolt. The batsman was helped from the field, his eyebrow coursing blood.

In the dressing-room a doctor stitched the gruesome wound. Wickets continued to fall. Denis said he would go out again. Elastoplast was put over the stitches. As a parting treatment the doctor gave the batsman – a very large brandy.

Denis went out and scored 145.

Hit Parade

Once again, I am giving up following boxing. Alas, I don't suppose it will last: Lenten abstinence from whisky only heightens anticipation for just-the-one on Easter Saturday evening. The drama and the ritual is all.

Professional prizefighting's genuflection to the chivalries of sport is offered only by the fighters themselves, who in my experience are invariably soft-tempered and fair folk. Their job is gruesomely stomach-turning and shamingly uncivilized. If it was banned I would not miss it one jot. Yet as long as it exists I suppose I will continue to waste weeks in my life travelling to boxing matches and pathetically reporting, indeed adding to, all the accompanying anticipation, the razz, the tazz and the seedy hype. The drama is the drug.

It was dramatic all right the other night at Wembley when two unconsidered American journeymen reached up and turned the lights off for two of the most carefully nursed, prospective British moneymakers in the 'game's' most lucrative divisions, the heavy and middleweight.

Frank Bruno's fall was that of a felled oak. As the dust settled there was a silence, and then followed the gentle rustle of falling leaves of greenbacks. Bruno's face was not the saddest in the stadium, I'm telling you. Though sorry it certainly was.

Faintin' Frank had signed on for the Flat Earth Society only an hour after Mark Kaylor, the middleweight champion. He was also seen to have had extremely skimpy schooling in the arts of self-defence. The fifth time Kaylor went down like a drunk trying to tie his shoe-laces, he stayed down for fully four minutes. Have you ever seen a plank twitching? It was grotesque of us to leave him there and run to interview the winner.

And all this only a matter of weeks after we had been sent personal copies of the latest, most definite and devastating report on boxing by the British Medical Association. One hitherto undiscovered paragraph of evidence offered by the BMA was the maximum long-term brain damage is caused to a boxer – for some now proven neurological reason – as he is *in the act of falling* to the canvas. Not when the blow itself melts the mandible. Nor even when the back of his skull meets the floor. But *as* he falls. At Wembley I was haunted by that paragraph.

Bruno had been far quicker to recover than the poor young Kaylor. I asked our toppled heavyweight if he had actually felt the blow that had made him senseless. He looked at me with big, honest, brown eyes and made a face as if I was daft. What of it, he seemed to be saying – 'Bugner got kayoed, Frazier got kayoed, Foreman got kayoed . . . I'll be back, don't worry.' That's what Ali used to say, I thought, and looked what happened to him.

I once had tea with Floyd Patterson in the Strand Palace Hotel. He was the first man ever to regain the world heavyweight title, but on the way suffered more indignities than, so far, has our Frankie, what with having to square up to the likes of Liston and Johannson.

This was Floyd on falling: 'You don't feel a thing. Honest. No pain at all. Sometimes I've gone down and it feels sweet as hell, like it must be the other guy falling, not you yourself. In a way it's a very lovable feeling. It might be like taking dope. Not that I've ever taken dope. But it might be what people tell me that's like – like you're floating, like you love everybody, like a hippie, I guess. But any actual pain, no sir.'

In the classic boxing memoir *In This Corner*, Jack Sharkey, the US heavy weight of half a century ago, also attempted to explain being kayoed: 'There is no pain, just a feeling of turmoil, momentum, constant buzzsaw going around. Like you're in a dream. Of course, when you snap out of it, that's when the shame comes. You snap out of it, you know you've lost and you are more or less ready to start crying.'

Sharkey, by the way, must have been quite a guy. He was the only fighter to bridge the legendary eras of Dempsey and Louis. He fought them both. He was once asked which was the hardest hitter? 'Dempsey hit me the hardest 'cos Dempsey hit me two hundred eleven thousand dollars' worth while Louis only hit me thirty-six thousand dollars' worth.' Which reminds me of another tale to lighten this grim piece. When Max Baer fought Louis, Dempsey was cornerman to Max. Quite early on into the party, Baer came back to his stool and Dempsey advised him not to worry ''cos he hasn't even hit you yet, kid'. Max turned dolefully to Dempsey and, through puffed and bloodstained lips, replied, 'Well, this next round you betta keep an eye on Arthur Donovan [the referee] 'cos some mutt in there is beatin' hell outa me!'

By coincidence, at Wembley, the cornerman and trainer to Bruno's opponent was Emile Griffith, one of the all-time greats who held two different world titles and altogether fought an astonishing twenty-four championship contests. Griffith is a charming, open, middle-aged man; he has kept money and marbles. Once he killed a man in the ring, Benny Paret on Lady Day, 1962, in the twelfth at Madison Square Garden.

I asked him about it: 'To tell you the truth, all I can remember was my manager (Gil Clancy), at the end of the eleventh round, slapping my face and saying, "Next time you got him hurt just keep punching till the referee stops it." That's what happened in the twelfth. Those words from Gil are the only thing I remember about the fight. I remember the weigh-in okay, when there was bad blood because he called me *maricon* which in English means "Faggot".'

'But of the fight itself I only remember Gil slapping me and shouting at me. What happened next I just can never put together, even all these years later. Maybe that's just the best way. Your mind just doesn't allow you to remember.'

Like the man said – next time you got him hurt, just keep punching till the referee stops it. Or till he doesn't, as the case may be.